Video Guide:
From How to Wow

M.-S. Göwecke

DATA BECKER®

Important Note

The procedures and programs described in this book are given regardless of patent. They are intended for amateur and training purposes only.

All information, technical specifications and programs in this book has been produced by the authors with the utmost care. However, the publishers can provide neither a guarantee, nor accept legal responsibility or any other responsibility, for consequences resulting from incorrect information.

The software and hardware designations and trademarks of companies used in this book shall generally remain subject to the legislation covering trade names, trademarks and protection under patent law.

The text contained in this book are suggestions and examples only. They include selective information only with no claims made for completeness.

In addition, although the text has been created with great care, the publisher and the authors shall accept no responsibility for the completeness or correctness, for the contents of the text or for the success of the users actions after following the information given in this manual. Using the information given in the text is solely at the user's own risk.

The names and addresses given in this text are fictitious. Any resemblance to persons alive or dead is purely coincidental and unintentional.

3. Processing the video material 83

4. From DVD to PC 127

Preface – From tape to disc

The medium of film has undergone enormous changes in every respect over the past few decades.

The first revolution happened with electronic image capturing, and we thought for a long time that this would not transcend the television screen.

The movie industry reacted to this new medium with new innovations such as "Cinemascope" and stereo sound to give cinema a quite specific appeal.

The film grain turned to bytes

Just as an amateur filmmaker would capture his home environment on Super 8 film 20 years ago, in the 90s he changed to video format, and used first Video8 or VHS and later Hi8 or SVHS tapes.

The second revolution, namely digitalization, also reached the video technology, and enabled almost anyone to capture images that were comparable to those taken with professional television cameras with small video cameras.

Camcorder meets PC

The incredible development in electronic entertainment is responsible also for the proliferation of a device which, in the era of Super 8, we could not imagine using for further processing of home movies: the computer.

Regarding video, the computer first took on the task of controlling very expensive image devices.

Swiftly shrinking sizes, paired with accelerating speed and a decrease in production costs resulted in the PC's becoming almost a standard of the home inventory.

In the meantime, video and computers have gotten so close that, ideally, when using MiniDV or Digital8, there is no need for any kind of "translation" (digitalization). The data stream of a video needs only to be copied onto the hard drive.

About writing onto discs

At the beginning of the 80s, digital technology led to the development of a completely new storage medium, the Compact Disc.

These were at first solely available as pre-recorded music CDs, but the advance of technology enabled us to buy blank silver discs and write data onto them with CD burners (which at the time were astronomically expensive) only a few years later.

Now such CD burners are nearly standard for any PC and can be bought for the same price as a CD player.

What in the beginning only applied to music has also become possible for film in recent years.

The idea was that what works with music must also be possible with movies.

Luckily, the potential of the CD was not yet exhausted. Musical data was stored on it entirely uncompressed, for the processors of yesteryear were running on all cylinders just to play back and transfer the digital signals. Additional decryption of compressed data in real time was thus out of the question (at least at a reasonable price).

As for the rest, the music CD has a playing time of 80 minutes, which is sufficient for saving an average music album.

To put a movie on such a disc meant to fit an additional second of film for every second of music (movie sound), if one wanted to keep to playing times similar to those of a music CD.

To realize this goal, it was therefore necessary to drastically reduce the amount of space taken up by the data.

As early as 1992, the MPEG-1 format was created, which made it possible to compress movies to a fraction of their original size.

Unlike the loss-free compression processes (everyone knows the ZIP format), the MPEG compression involves a *loss-ridden reduction process*.

In essence, the process tries to omit data deemed "insignificant" to our eyes and ears.

On the basis of MPEG-1, the video CD (or CD I) was born, which is the predecessor of today's DVD.

1. VirtualDub as a freeware recorder

Windows itself is not very well equipped to import video files, thus additional software has to be used. Those afraid that this will mean buying another program need not worry.

In the video processing sector in particular there is a large number of software tools available as freeware: VirtualDub is one of these and thus offers all of its features for free.

This capturing program – already considered a classic – captures video images and offers a range of useful features.

For example, in the recording of long video excerpts, it can circumvent the very restricting size limit of video files by simply cutting the video stream into several blocks of determinable size.

As if this weren't enough, VirtualDub can even change the hard drive or the partition as soon as it is full. Seamless capturing of 30 GB of material on two 20 GB drives is thus no problem.

1.1 Technical requirements

To capture video with a PC, you need certain minimum specifications. Not so long ago, you needed a high end PC to deal with time-critical issues like video capturing. Now any supermarket PC can cope with them.

Nevertheless, there are certain minimum requirements necessary, which we will address more closely in the following.

The image must be in the PC

Before a video image can be captured it must be in the PC. To facilitate access for programs like VirtualDub, the PC must have a video interface based on Video for Windows.

You have the following options:

Graphics cards with Video-in

In most cases, no additional card is necessary, especially if the graphics card on your computer has Video-in.

If you find one or more connections named "AV-In", "Video-In", "Video Line-In" or "S-Video-In" near the monitor connection, things look good, and you may not need an additional video card.

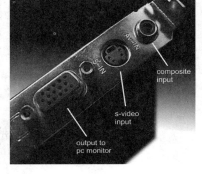

However, the video card only looks after the image. A sound card is thus absolutely necessary, but it doesn't cost very much these days.

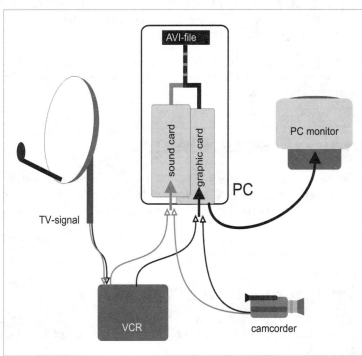

TV cards

Before you toy with the idea of getting a new graphics card ...

If your graphics card has been manufactured recently, throwing it out may be a waste of money, unless your card doesn't have a Video-in socket. Instead, consider adding further functions and opt for a TV card.

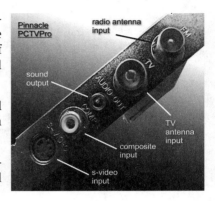

If you have an antenna/cable/satellite connection, such a card with TV tuner facilitates the reception of TV programs and the playing of video from other sources over the specified connections.

Depending on the model, an additional sound card may be needed, so that the sound can be recorded at the same time.

A strong advantage: the received TV programs can be recorded to the hard drive and made into video CDs.

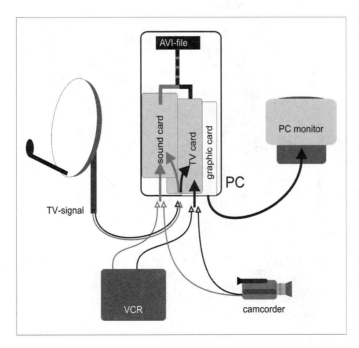

Video capture cards

Another variant of video input is a video capture card with analog inputs.

Such cards offer a wide range of features and cost approximately $100. However, you can also easily spend a couple of thousand dollars on one.

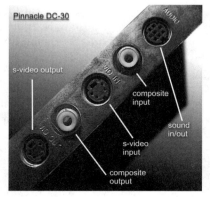

For those who primarily want to capture their own video images and burn them onto CDs, a special video capture board is probably the best solution.

You don't even have to sacrifice TV capturing. To record TV images you can tap into the signal through most video recorder output channels.

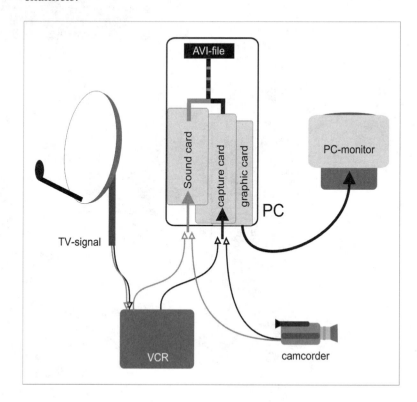

Faster, bigger – the hard drives

Video files need a lot of space.

Even with compression processes, recording an hour of good quality video may take up 10 GB.

In the meantime, however, hard drives have become quite affordable and offer a lot of space.

Thanks to modern transfer standards like UDMA-100, inexpensive IDE drives can also cope with the data stream.

Install the drivers carefully!

It is always advised to optimize the performance of the hard drive by installing the bus master driver for the mainboard, which provides for a constant data transfer between the components, in this case the graphics/TV or video cards.

If your PC has been used previously only for Office applications, you will become aware of the system weaknesses and driver problems during such demanding activities as recording videos.

1.2 Running VirtualDub

VirtualDub does not have a setup routine like most other programs.

You simply have to copy the directory to a desired position, usually in the default folder *Programs*.

1.3 Determining the speed of the hard drive

For video capture with PCs, the speed of the hard drive is of the essence, as it determines the quality of the captured images. The data transfer rate is also important here, for it informs you how many files per second can be written. The higher the number, the faster the drive.

With the help of an additional program, VirtualDub can test the performance of the hard drive and determine the data transfer rate.

The program *AuxSetup* can be found in the VirtualDub directory. For better access, we advise you right-click on the program icon to create a shortcut on the desktop (*Send to/Desktop...*):

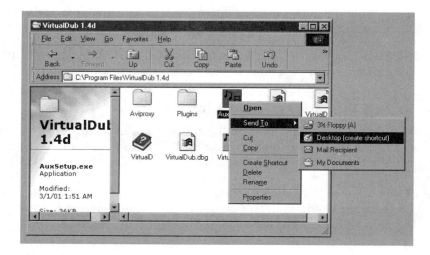

After starting the Setup tool, the following window will appear, in which you can gain access to the *Disk performance test* by clicking the *Benchmark* button:

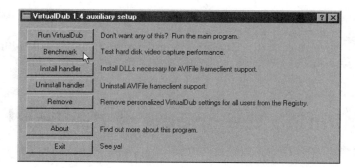

The subsequent dialog box can determine the performance properties of the relevant hard drive:

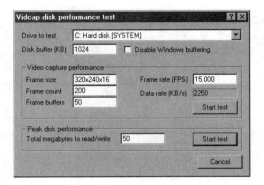

Regardless of what is to be tested – first, you must select the relevant drive:

Here you can determine the size of the buffer memory which balances out fluctuations in the data stream. If the drive should slow down and not save the relevant data immediately, the latter can be transferred temporarily to a buffer memory (a reserved area in the memory), which prevents data loss.

Windows also has a system for buffering data streams, which can be disabled by checking *Disable Windows buffering*.

A larger buffer area is better, but in that case the hard drive needs to be fast enough to process the amounts of data that arrive there. Otherwise, even the biggest cache memory will "overflow".

Hard disk tests

VirtualDub has two ways of determining hard drive performance, the second of which provides more practical and comprehensible results in the field *Peak disk performance*.

For the sake of completeness, however, we also want to mention the first method:

Test1: Video capture performance

With this test you can determine whether certain data transfer rates can be sustained by the system.

Determining the data transfer rate considers only uncompressed data without paying attention to compressions. Similarly, you can only enter the frame size (in pixels) followed by the color depth of every pixel (in bits) in the *Frame Size* field.

We have selected here the values of a typical NTSC TV screen as test values:

If this value – the frame size – is multiplied by the number of frames per second (*Frame rate*: 25.000), you obtain the *Data rate* (here a full 20 Mbytes).

The length of the test can be determined by the *Frame count* – here a time of 400 single frames has been set (= 16 seconds).

Basically, the longer the test, the more accurate and significant the result.

In the *Frame buffers* field, the number of image-buffers is given (see page 19).

Clicking on *Start test* produces the following result after 16 seconds:

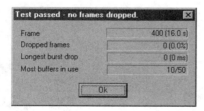

Just the way it should be – not a single image was lost.

Test 2: Peak disk performance

A more useful method is to measure the maximum data output of the hard drive.

The principle is simple: a test file is written and read. The time necessary for this informs us about the performance.

After you have entered the size of the test file, you can begin:

Here, too, the bigger the test file, the more reliable the result:

With such a result, there should be no problems with capturing.

Test results:

The aforementioned tests help you determine the maximum data throughput of your computer.

It is advised not to think of this value as the definitive one, as test procedures lasting a relatively short time can only provide approximate results.

Thus, keep your settings below the values obtained in order to avoid as much image loss as possible.

1.4 How to record?

Double-clicking on *VirtualDub.exe* launches the program and this start screen.

1. VirtualDub as a freeware recorder

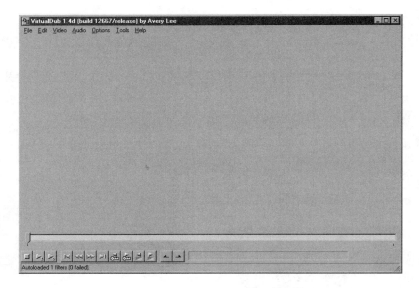

The empty screen may surprise you but this is quite normal.

After starting, you will find yourself in the part of the program that deals with processing video clips, i.e. where they can be edited, converted or filtered.

The "recording studio" hides behind the *File/Capture AVI...* menu item:

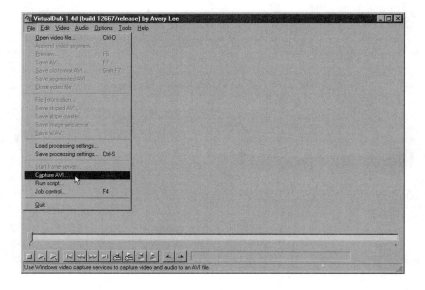

In order for VirtualDub to "find" the video image in your PC and record it, the hardware that is providing the image must be compatible with Video for Windows and have the relevant drivers, which is the case, however, for most TV or video cards.

Some cards have their own, incompatible drivers, but most are (semi-)professional interface cards, like Matrox RT2000.

If VirtualDub has no drivers available which are compatible with Video for Windows, a warning message will appear.

If your hardware should have such drivers, according to the manufacturer's information, then read the relevant manuals and install the hardware again, if necessary.

If there are no problems, the capturing window of VirtualDub will appear.

Only a blue/green screen instead of an image?

Ideally, the video signal should then appear in the window, be it the image from the TV card, the video recorder, or the connected camcorder.

Sometimes only a blue or green window appear.

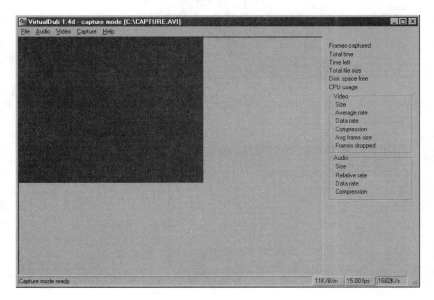

But don't worry: Usually, a blue screen is displayed if a capturing driver but no image has been found.

When the program is first started, it is generally necessary to tweak a few basic settings to determine how something is to be recorded and to where.

Usually, this procedure will also uncover the causes for the lack of an image.

1.5 VirtualDub's default settings

Before capturing can begin, a few settings have to be tweaked in the program. You can save these settings, so that you only have to do this once.

Determining the capture disk or file

Capturing a video clip involves several megabytes of data. VirtualDub can determine the drive and the directory where capturing should be made so that different projects will not get mixed up.

Select *File/Set capture file...*

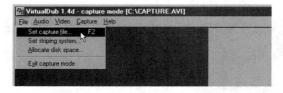

After selecting the drive and the directory you can then leave the file selection dialog box.

If at all possible, you should not record on the default drive C, as in most cases this is where Windows has been installed.

Windows itself constantly saves momentarily unnecessary content in so-called temporary files that are usually placed on the hard drive.

The less RAM a PC has, the more often such writing and reading activities will occur.

If you are capturing video on the same drive, the writing/reading devices have to cope with two processes simultaneously and constantly switch between temporary and video files, which can lead to image loss and can cause crashes.

Ideally, a second hard drive would be used to save video files.

Video and audio settings

Both video and audio files should be compressed when captured, otherwise you would have to deal with huge amounts of data.

Selecting the sound format

Under *Audio/Compression...* you can select an audio compressor.

Here we select the ADPCM compression.

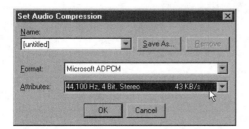

Compared to the standard PCM format, which is also used for audio CDs (44,1KHz, 16 Bit, Stereo), the compressed ADPCM variant uses only a quarter of the space (43 KB/s instead of 172 KB/s).

For those of the opinion that such small data rates would not save much space:

If you think that 74 minutes of PCM sound with an audio CD can take up approximately 650 MB (the typical blank CD), then it is clear that when recording a movie of this length you could save almost 490 MB using ADPCM.

Regulating the sound

If something goes wrong with the recording, it is difficult to iron it out during a later editing process.

An optimal sound level provides for the best possible distortion range.

The loudest sounds should not be over-steered, otherwise the signal would be distorted. On the other hand, you should not use a level that is too low.

When in doubt, it is better to be too low than too high, as the very large dynamic capacity of 16 bit sound (i.e. the ability to record very quiet as well as very loud sounds) forgives a low level. No digital sound format will tolerate sound distortion, however.

VirtualDub has a built-in module for displaying the current sound level that can be opened by going to *Audio/Volume meter*.

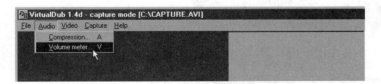

The launched window is simple and functional:

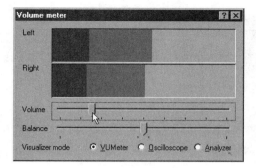

The *Volume meter* window is composed essentially from the blue-red sound level indicator and the meters for volume and balance.

If a mono sound is selected under *Audio/Compression...*, only one channel is displayed.

Set the volume slider to a position where the loudest sounds to be recorded are almost at the maximum volume level.

In addition to the sound level display, there are also two other possibilities to view the volume:

The oscilloscope display also shows an image of the sound level, only in time.

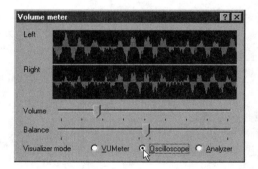

The frequency analysis dialog box that opens under *Analyser* can be quite re-vealing, for it displays the current frequencies of the signal:

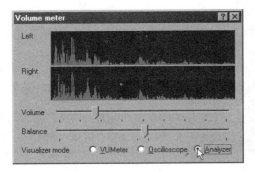

The signal here shows a high bass level, for example.

Selecting the Video-in

Now we want to make the pesky blue window disappear. The blue window usually means that the Video-in has not been selected correctly.

The menu option *Video/Source...* will clarify this:

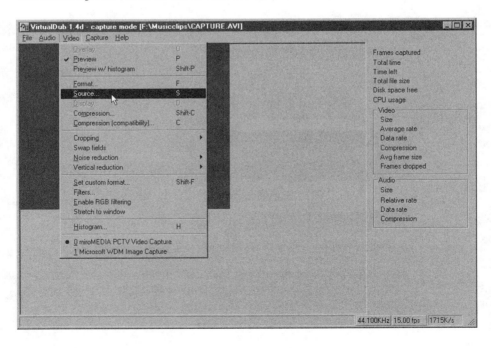

The TV card used here (Pinnacle PCTV Pro) was set to *Composite* (Line-in), and as no device was connected there, the blue screen appeared.

Clicking on *Tuner* connects the TV signal of the receiver to the card, and this appears immediately in the main window:

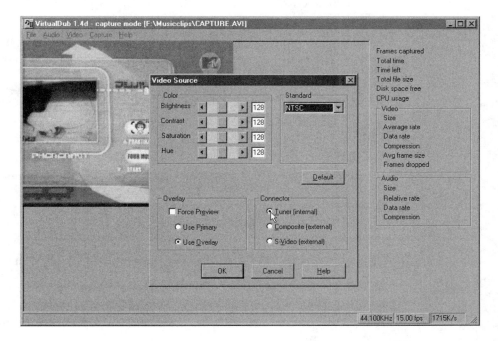

The setting options in this dialog box depend completely on the hardware used.

Features like type and number of Video-ins or the image parameters available can also be found here.

The individual areas:

Setting the color, contrast & color saturation

With the three sliders, you can set the *Brightness*, *Contrast* and *Saturation* for the active Video-in.

The adjustments are shown in real time in the main window.

Selecting the TV standard

Here you must select the TV standard used. In the USA we use NTSC, in Germany, the standard is PAL and, in France SECAM.

Setting the overlay

By "Overlay" we mean the way the video image is shown on the computer monitor.

This "foreign" signal can be integrated ("overlaid") into the current image in different ways, depending on the capabilities of the PC's graphics card.

With this card, there are three modes available. Should there be problems with displaying the video image on the computer monitor, adjustments could prove helpful. If your driver does not support overlay settings, you can only use the corresponding VirtualDub menu option, *Video/Overlay*. With serious problems, you can go back to the uncomplicated (choppy) Preview mode (*Video/Preview*).

The *Force Preview* mode ensures the best possible compatibility, because it can function with any VGA graphics card. The images from the TV card are diverted through the memory, from where they are forwarded to the memory of the graphics card at regular intervals. This may mean, however, that the image on the monitor is not constant.

With *Use Primary*, the TV card creates the scaled image and transports it directly to the graphics card memory.

The setting *Use Overlay* then enables the graphics card to exclusively take care of displaying the video image, provided that the card supports this option. For video capture, this means disburdening the main processor that can now dedicate itself to compressing the video image.

Choosing signal in

This TV card has two other Video-in options in addition to the actual tuner to which you can connect a video recorder or camcorder.

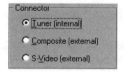

Should the device have an S-video-out and – as here – a corresponding in channel, you should select the composite signal, because the image quality is visibly better due to the separate transfer of brightness and color values.

Selecting the video format

The format of the video to be captured should be selected with care, as it determines the quality and the space used by the file created.

The video format incorporates three parameters:

1. The pixel measurements of the image.

2. The image format (colorspace).

3. The compression format.

You can reach the settings by going to *Video/Format...*:

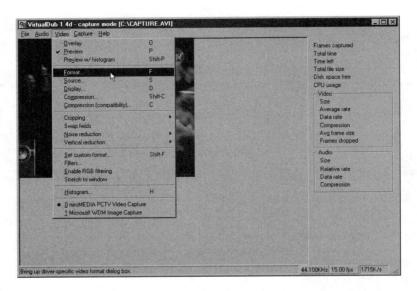

Here you can also find the options that the hardware drivers provide.

With PCTV Pro this dialog box appears:

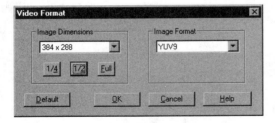

The video format is made up of the measurements of the image and the image format.

1. Selecting the image dimensions

With *Image Dimensions*, you can determine the image dimensions.

Which video format you choose depends primarily on the purpose of the image.

We want to create a standard video CD from the material captured. The minimum size should be the resolution, i.e. 352 x 240 pixels, a format that can be handled even by the "small" cards. Thus, you see how a video CD can be created without using complex hardware.

The default setting of PCTV Pro is a frame size of 384 x 288 pixels. To spare the MPEG encoder the trouble of converting the horizontal resolution from 384 to 352 and the vertical resolution from 288 to 240 later (which can lead to image deterioration), the video CD should be recorded in the latter resolution:

With most cards, there are different image dimensions available.

2. Setting the colorspace/image format

The quality and size of the data depend on how the analog TV image was scanned during digitalization.

The relevant image formats can be found in the list field and are usually described in the graphics, TV or video card manual.

In our example, the setting *YUV2* provides the best quality.

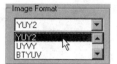

3. Adjusting the video compression settings

Because capturing video involves huge amounts of data, you must use precious hard disk space sparingly even at the beginning of digital image processing and reduce the amount of data of a digital video.

Compressors offer the solution to this in the form of certain small "instructions" on how to encrypt image and sound contents so that they take up less space (coding).

To play back, the image has to go through the reverse process: decompression makes the image visible again (decoding).

Such "instructions" are also named *codecs* (from *co*ding/*dec*oding) and are either integrated into the hardware so that they can be executed by special processors (hardware codecs) or are small software modules that can be installed on the system (software codecs).

For the most well-known formats like MJPEG (Motion JPEG), MPEG, Indeo and DV, there can be different codecs from different manufacturers.

The TV card used here installs the codec Indeo 5.10 (in addition to the drivers) to compress video images.

Selection is made in a special dialog box that can be launched by going to *Video/ Compression....*

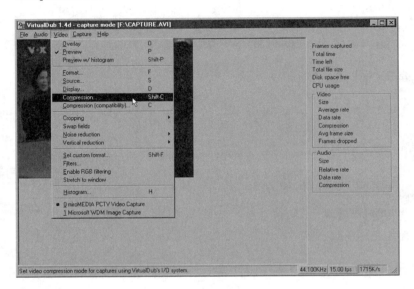

The following shows the number of codecs for the relevant driver:

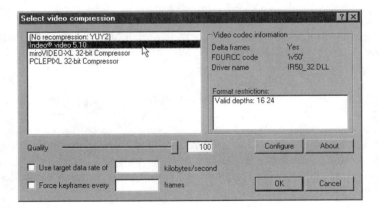

This is not a complete list of codecs installed on the system, but simply a selection of those with which capturing is possible.

As this TV card is suitable for use with the Indeo codec, we will select the latter.

With the slider below ...

... you can select the configuration quality of the codec.

The farther to the right you set the slider, the better the image quality and the higher the data transfer rate.

Depending on the purpose of use, it is advised that test capturing be carried out with different settings to get a feel of the quality and quantity of date to be expected from a position on the slide bar.

The *Custom format*

Should the desired capture format not exist, it can be set manually in many cases (depending on whether your hardware supports it) by going to *Video/ Set custom format*:

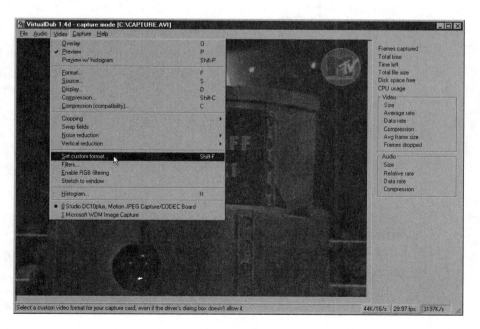

In this way, the video card can be used to record in another image dimension:

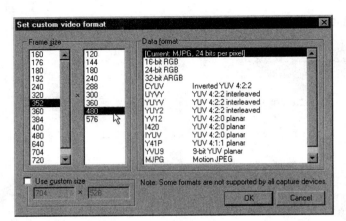

Additionally, you can select a certain image format on the right side. If the card doesn't support this, a warning message will appear when capturing starts.

This principle of capturing only one of the image frames in full resolution makes for a good compromise between image size and quality, as all other image information will provide for a better result when converted into the desired format later.

The currently "unnaturally" proportioned image should not alarm you because it represents only a temporary stage in our process. If it is processed further into an MPEG-4 movie, the desired resolution will adapt to the proportions.

That distorted video files can later become "normal" images is exemplified by creating MPEG-1 or MPEG-2 files for (Super-) video CDs.

So, for example, the pixel format from SVCD, which is visibly distorted, namely 480 x 480 pixels, is then brought to the right dimensions by the hardware of the DVD player when it plays it back.

The typical recording: Codecs

In addition to the aforementioned Indeo 5.10, the formats used in video capturing are MJPEG and (more and more often) MPEG.

MJPEG (Motion JPEG)

The classical photo compression format JPEG has been further developed to a video compression format and was successfully installed in the first analog video interface cards.

In this process, all individual frames of a video are compressed and saved in sequence as video files.

As with the JPEG format, not too much compression can lead to almost loss-free capture, which is of course bought at the price of a larger amount of hard disk space being taken up (at least 5 MB/sec of video file is required).

MJPEG offers a relatively good image with very slow data transfer rates.

MPEG-1/MPEG-2

Newer TV cards can capture directly in MPEG format, which ideally requires no more conversion when creating video or Super video CDs from the captured images.

MPEG-1, as the elder standard, displays usable images with relatively slow data transfer rates and a quarter of the TV resolution, and is still commonplace across Asia in the form of video CDs.

MPEG-2 is an enhancement of MPEG-1. It tends towards slow data transfer rates and congestion. In this respect it is inferior to MJPEG. On the other hand, better image results are produced with slower data transfer rates, as we can see in one area of its use – DVDs. In the meantime, more and more video editing systems are using MPEG-2.

Further "settings" before the first recording

Now all should be prepared for the first recording.

In the bottom right corner of the capture window of VirtualDub, you can find the Quick Menu, in which the most important parameters can be viewed:

You can see here that the frame rate is 15 fps (frames per second); thus, the number of images to be recorded per second does not correspond to the frame rate of our TV system (29.97 fps).

Frame rates

There are two frame rates for TV signals worldwide: 29.97 frames per second with NTSC (e. g. in the US), 25 frames per second with PAL (e.g. in Germany) and SECAM (e. g. in France).

With this Quick Menu, you can change the values by clicking on the mouse.

To adjust the frame rate:

One click on the frame rate button ...

... opens a table, from which *29.97 fps* is selected:

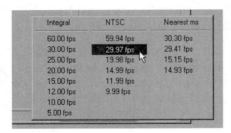

The menu option *Capture/Settings...* contains some additional settings:

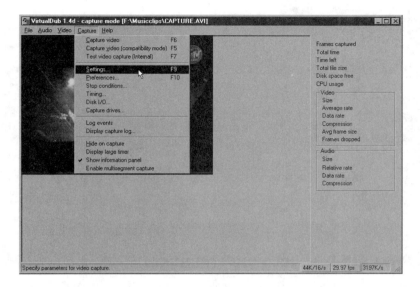

In the dialog field, options can be set which affect the actual capturing process:

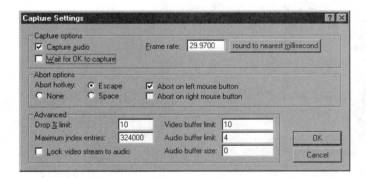

First, a small checkmark determines whether sound is to be recorded or not.

If yes, *Capture audio* must be checked.

The *Wait for OK to capture* option introduces a window that you must confirm when you start capturing.

The *Frame rate* changed previously in the Quick menu can also be changed numerically here.

In the *Abort options* area at the bottom, you can determine which (mouse) button can abort the capture:

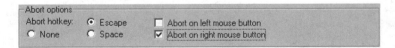

In our example, pressing the Esc button or right-clicking the mouse aborts the capturing process.

The Advanced options should be left alone.

VirtualDub saves your settings ...

Obviously you do not have to make these settings again every time you start the program ...

The achieved state can be saved as the default to be used every time the program starts.

Select *Capture/Preferences...*:

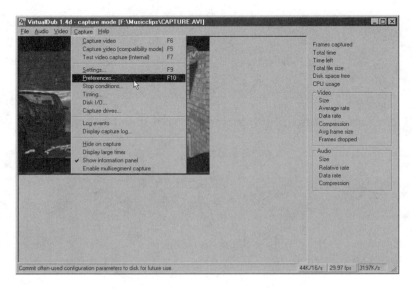

In the corresponding dialog box ...

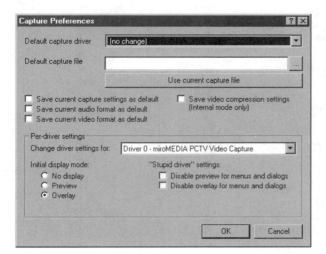

... enable all *Save...*-Options:

Done.

1.6 Capturing in VirtualDub

Now we can really start the fun.

We want to record a music video from TV.

VirtualDub supports two recording modes:

The *compatibility mode* leaves the actual recording to the system's own Video for Windows and ensures functioning with most capture cards.

When using the internal capture mode, VirtualDub takes care of all the capturing. One of the advantages is that it can create an adaptive data transfer rate, meaning that a data transfer rate can be suited to the image content. This saves space.

Both modes are used regularly and appear twice in the menus. The compatibility mode is indicated by *(compatibility)* or *(compatibility mode)*:

The compression can be selected separately for each mode:

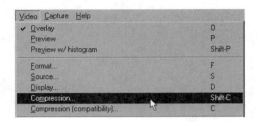

You can select the mode even when capturing:

For the following capture procedure, the internal capture mode is used. If problems should arise, e.g. if images are lost during capture, the compatibility mode can always be used.

Attention, capturing!

Start capturing by going to *Capture/Capture video*. Alternatively, you can press F6:

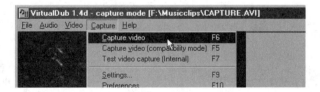

It's happening. Capturing has started.

Information, information, information ...

During capturing, VirtualDub keeps you up-to-date by displaying a wealth of data on the right hand side of the capturing screen:

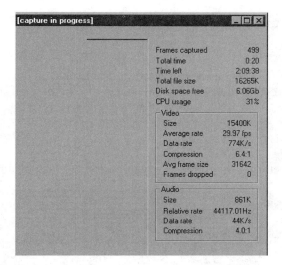

The following values are particularly interesting:

- *Time left*, just like *Disk space free*, shows the space still available on the relevant drive. The display in hours, minutes and seconds is much more descriptive.

- In the *Video* category, the *data rate* is constantly displayed. If capturing in the compatibility mode, the number does not change, because you are working with a fixed data transfer rate. In the internal capture mode, you can see how the data transfer rate is made suitable to the complexity of the image.

- Also in the *Video* category, you can find *Frames dropped* which counts the frames that have not been captured in the drive, thus causing jerks in the recorded video.

In such a case, changes must be made to the video and audio settings. The root of the problem can be a data transfer rate that was set to high or a slow or poorly configured hard drive.

And ... cut!

Capturing can be aborted as determined in the capture settings (see page 40).

Afterwards, we can see the live image as before.

New capture, new file!

Now you must pay attention!

If another capturing procedure has been started, then VirtualDub overwrites the clip just saved, as the clip is always captured under the file defined in *File/Set capture file*

The following method is tried and tested:

1 The capturing directory is displayed as a window next to VirtualDub.

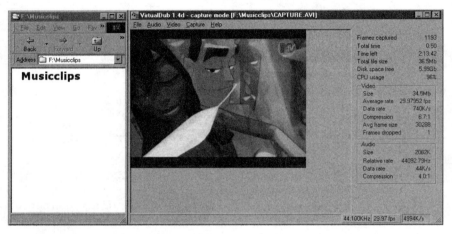

2 Go to *File/Set capture file*, and select the file *capture.avi* as the capture file.

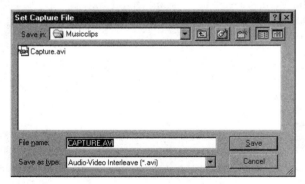

3 After the first clip has been recorded, *capture.avi* appears in the neighboring window, and you can change its name.

4 Now you can resume capturing. After each capture, a *capture.avi* is created. Rename it, etc.

1.7 If it takes longer: AVI files bigger than 2 or 4 GB

If only short music videos were to be captured onto disk, as in the previous example, there would be no problem.

With an average data transfer rate of 700-1000 KB per second, the gravity of the situation only becomes apparent after 20 minutes: the AVI file created reaches 2 GB.

2 GB – a problem ...

Video for Windows has since its introduction limited its hard drive partitions to 2 GB, which is also the maximum file size achievable (including for AVI files).

This was an almost impossibly large size for a video file at the time, since the only comparison were tiny movies around then the size of a stamp. Videos on home computers had not been thought of.

But the times changed, and when you convert to the digital consumer format MiniDV, the aged AVI reaches its limit after approximately 12 minutes.

By extending the file system from FAT16 to FAT32 the limit for these files increases from 2 to 4 GB (the partitions can become even larger). The latest version of Windows 95 (OSR 2) and Windows 98 support the FAT32 file system.

The special NTFS file system in Windows NT and in its successor, Windows 2000, recognizes such limitations only in the terabyte area, which will not become a serious obstacle in the future.

... and the solution

VirtualDub can facilitate capturing long segments even with Windows 95 – provided there is enough hard disk space – thanks to its *Multisegment capturing*.

The principle is simple to imagine:

Once the capture file reaches a certain size (which is freely defined), it is then closed very quickly and a new one is opened. If no more space is available in the hard drive or partition, VirtualDub can change to the next one.

Step by step:

Movies as multiple segments: *Multisegment capturing* in VirtualDub

Only a few settings are essentially necessary to effectively handle the file size limit.

Defining the capturing hard drive

Here we select the menu entry *Capture drives...* under *Capture:*

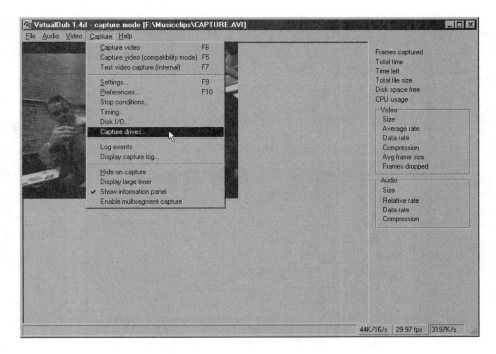

The rest of the process depends on the hard drives available to you.

All necessary settings can be adjusted in the dialog box *Spill System Setup*:

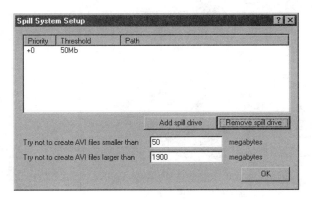

For example, imagine your PC has two hard drives:

In the first drive, there are partitions C and E, whereby the system is on C as usual. Partition E is for general data storage.

Another, faster drive is divided into partitions D and F, and is supposed to be used primarily for storing videos.

Enter the following in the dialog box:

1 First, click on *Path* and find the path to a desired (existing) directory.

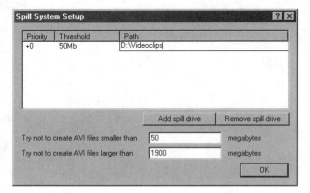

2 With the *Add spill drive* button you can add drives:

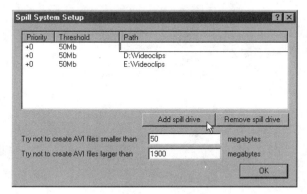

3 Partitions D and F should take priority, as they are on the fast drive, while E should only be used in an emergency.

In *Priority* you can rank the capture drives. The higher the number, the more likely it will be used for capturing.

If two drives have the same value, the drive with the most free space is the first choice.

The priority for E should be set to 1 with the mouse, meaning that this partition is only used when the two faster drives are completely full:

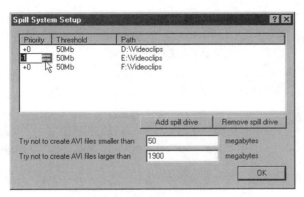

The value in *Threshold* determines at which amount of remaining space the drive should be changed. This value can be increased up to 127 MB.

With the *Remove spill drive* button, a defined and selected drive can be removed at the click of a mouse.

Finally, you can set the limit values for the files to be created in the entry fields at the bottom.

The first parameter is the threshold value, which ensures that files below a certain size are not created.

The second number is the maximum size of the video file. The 1900 MB entered here ensure that a new file is created before the old one exceeds the 2 GB limit.

Important: the standard file must now be placed on one of the fast drives in an appropriate directory.

You can select the appropriate directory quickly by going to *File/Set capture file...*:

Enabling the spill system

After you have closed the dialog box, the defined spill system must be enabled.

This is done by checking the menu option *Capture/Enable multisegment capture.*

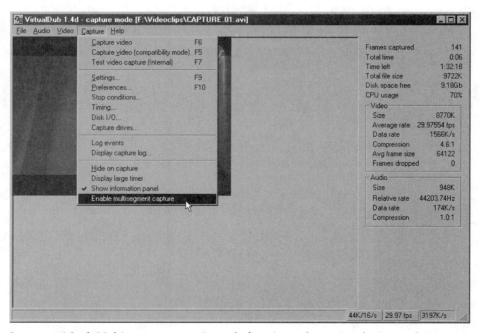

Important! Such Multisegment capturing only functions when using the internal capture mode (Capture/Capture video).

The compatibility mode does not support this feature, because such functions have not been integrated into Video for Windows!

The files created are assigned a number according to the following sequence and are handled like one file by VirtualDub:

- clipname.00.avi
- clipname.01.avi
- clipname.02.avi
- ...

In editing programs, these AVI blocks can be arranged in sequence so as to recreate the original movie.

To minimize possible problems, it is advised not to carry out audio compression during capture but to use the PCM format instead.

For formatting the image, compressors like MJPEG are the first choice, for they work without key frames and thus ensure the best file transfer keeping the exact image.

On the other hand, some formats save one image (key frame), and then for a number of subsequent images only save changes to this keyframe. This principle is used above all with MPEG formats (see also page 206).

1.8 No space – what then?

After successful capturing, the capture drive may well be full.

If a data transfer rate of a mere 800 KB per second was used, a 90 minute long movie will take up 4.3 GB.

If you want to burn this onto CDs, you will need 6 to 7 blank CDs and will have to change discs every 15 minutes – not very convenient ...

Now we can use VirtualDub's ability as a data converter, because choosing the definitive format is only limited by the number of codecs installed.

Find the best compression procedures for the image and sound. VirtualDub can then create finished AVI files. Here image and sound can be interwoven or saved as separate files.

Codecs – where can you find them?

A codec is an "instruction" about how to code video or sound files so that they use less space. Usually, it also includes how to make a video movie out of an encrypted data stream (decoding).

We have already used such a codecs for the video capture (see page 33), its most important role being to compress the video stream in real time.

Most capture codecs work symmetrically, which means that the time to encode is about the same as the time to decode. Capture and playback are possible in real time.

The asymmetric codecs are different: they take more time to encode but can be decoded in real time, i.e. played back.

The advantages of this asymmetric coding are evident: images created with it are clearly smaller because they are not processed under time pressure, which makes more complex processing procedures possible.

Owing to ever increasing PC performance, such differences will not be as significant in the future, when it will be possible to achieve the 25 frames per second required by real time even when faced with mathematically complex image calculations.

Now, after the video has been saved on the drive, all of the other steps are not time-critical, meaning that one of the aforementioned asymmetric codecs can be used.

Of course, the highest aim of the programmer of such codecs is to ensure the video created is of brilliant quality and does not take up any more space.

Thanks to codecs such as MPEG-2 we can now watch entire movies on data carriers like the DVD.

Windows has some of its own codecs, like Indeo or Cinepak, already installed.

Other formats, like Apple Quicktime, which comes with many codecs, can be acquired separately or are parts of other software products, like video editing programs.

Additional hardware like TV or interface cards can install their own codecs on your system, which can then normally be used by programs like VirtualDub.

Some companies, like Mainconcept, offer their own codecs independent of any product.

MPEG-4 and its offspring

Just as the audio format MP3 has become standard, a similar development looks likely for video with MPEG-4.

Originally, the corresponding codec was developed by Microsoft for the ASF web format and was supplied with the Media Player.

Similarly, with the encoding program *Media Tools*, it was only possible to create MPEG-4 videos as ASF but not as AVI.

The consequence was that these codecs soon became hacker tools.

So after a short while, a new codec appeared on the video scene called *DivX;-)*. You should enjoy this codec with great caution, however, for your enjoyment may have legal consequences. On the one hand, there are grounds to assume parts of the original MPEG-4 codec from Microsoft were "converted" for DivX, on the other, some versions include the MP3codec from the Fraunhofer Institute, which is patent fraud.

DivX is used as any other normal codec and is supported by many software platforms. With the help of the Internet, advanced current versions are always in circulation and are widespread.

A newer variant called *OpenDivX* should be completely legal, however, thanks to its entirely new programming. Microsoft has also not expressed any opposition against it thus far.

Home users are rarely deterred from such illegal codecs, and, thanks to search engines, you do not have to be an expert to find them on the Internet.

Codec installation

Because a codec is not an actual program, we must ask how these "codes" are placed on our computers.

1. OpenDivX

The OpenDivX codec included in the book's CD-Rom is conveniently packed in a single file and almost installs itself after double clicking on it.

All files are automatically unpacked and put in the correct place.

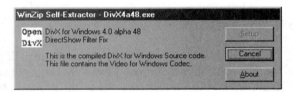

In the end, everything seems the same. Some entries were made in Windows, however, which enable programs like VirtualDub to access this codec so that it can be selected as the output format.

2. DivX

The variants of DivX codecs can be installed on a PC relatively easily as well.

We want to demonstrate the steps of the installation with the help of version 3.11a.

On starting the executable file, the following message appears on the screen:

Then a dialog box appears, in which the file path for the data to be copied can be determined:

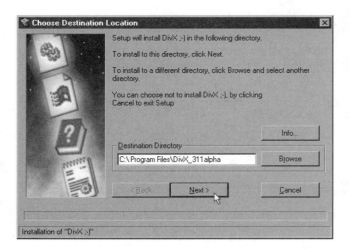

Now all relevant files are unpacked and copied into the relevant directory.

The following window opens automatically.

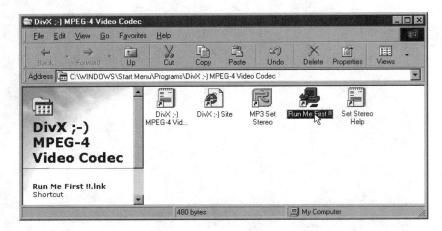

Significantly, the file *Run Me First!!* must be started first, because it starts the actual installation procedure:

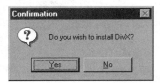

Confirming with Yes allows the procedure to be implemented and completed automatically.

Removing codecs – uninstalling

Not all of the codecs must remain on your computer forever.

If you discover you have installed one of the illegal ones, you may wish to remove it from your system as quickly as possible.

Essentially, there are two options for uninstalling unwanted codecs:

1. The authors of the software have anticipated uninstallation and provided for it in Windows.

2. Find the codec in the Control Panel and remove it manually.

Both procedures can be carried out quickly.

1. Checking for an existing uninstalling routine

Like the OpenDivX codec, many other software products offer the option of installing and uninstalling under *Software* in the Control Panel, which saves endlessly searching for the installed item.

The first step should always be (as with other software) to search for an entry in the Windows Control Panel.

This is opened by going to *Start/Settings/Control Panel*:

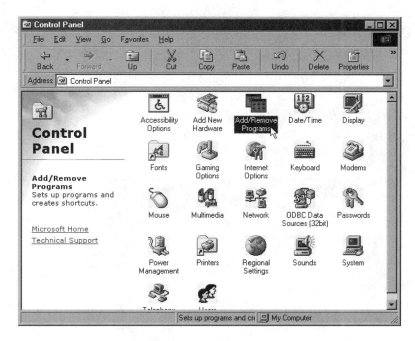

By double-clicking on *Add/Remove Programs*, a list appears including all programs that can be uninstalled.

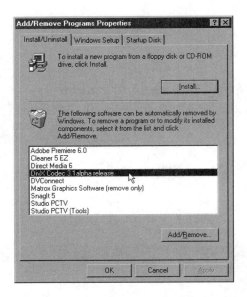

A double click on the codec is enough to remove it.

2. Manually "kicking out" codecs

The first port of call is again the Control Panel (*Start/Settings/Control Panel*). Double-click on the *Multimedia* icon:

In the subsequent window, you will find all currently installed codecs in the *Devices* tab under *Video Compression Codecs*.

Select the codec to be removed by clicking on it and selecting *Properties*:

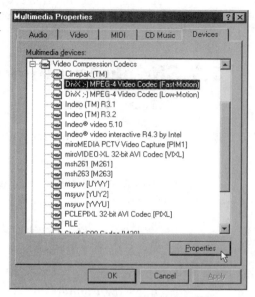

Now, simply click on *Remove* ...

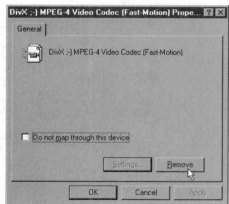

... and confirm the procedure:

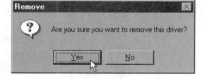

The codec is removed from the list.

A system restart may be required.

Please remember that this procedure only removes the actual codec files. Additional data such as Readme files or similar files are not removed.

1.9 Shrinking movies – Exporting in VirtualDub

After this brief encounter with video codecs, OpenDivX should be installed on your computer.

We would now like to use it to make the size of a captured music video more practical.

All necessary steps are carried out in the video processing mode, the "starting point" of VirtualDub.

If video clips have just been digitized, the capture mode can be changed by going to *File/Exit capture mode*:

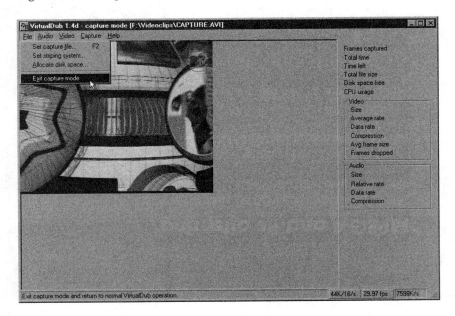

First go to *File/Open video file...* to load the clip to be processed:

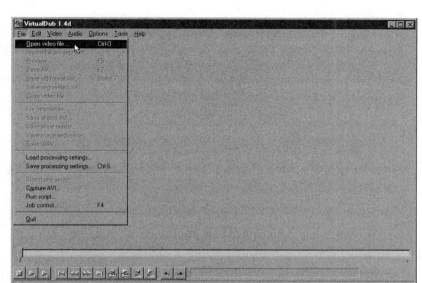

If two empty frames appear at first, move the slider below to display the video:

The image on the left side always shows the original, while the right shows the results of the process used so that they can be assessed.

Defining the starting and ending points

In the processing window, you have the option of marking the video clip, thereby defining new starting and ending points.

If you want to digitize music videos from television, as in the example, start capturing from the introduction and keep capturing until after the end of the clip.

Subsequent editing to the right length can then be carried out in VirtualDub:

1 Moving towards the future starting point. With the slider, you can control the relevant position at least roughly.

For a single frame position, the relevant button can then be used.

In this way, you can isolate the exact first frame of a music video:

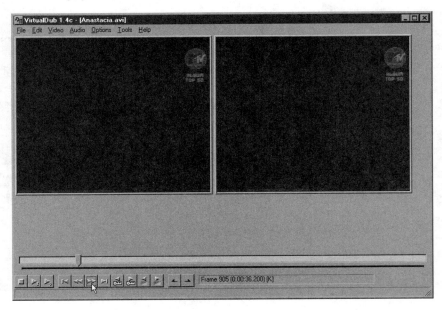

2 This position can then be marked with the *In-Point* button.

3 The ending point is marked in the same way. The marked area appears in black.

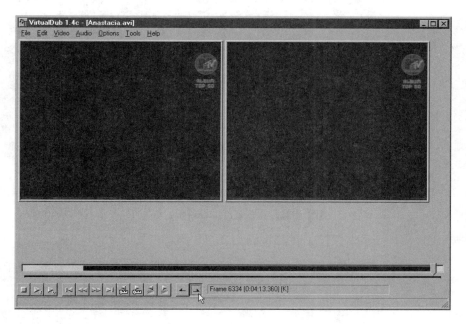

Processing mode and codec selection

After you have determined to the exact frame which sections are to be exported, you must select the codecs (the selection occurs separately for image and sound).

Setting the processing mode

The prospective video should only differ from the original in space needed, meaning that each individual frame should be decompressed in an RGB frame before being reduced further with a new codec. In order for VirtualDub to really do this, enable the *Full processing mode* menu option in the *Video* menu. With *Direct stream copy*, the video files would be copied unchanged without incorporating the parameters set.

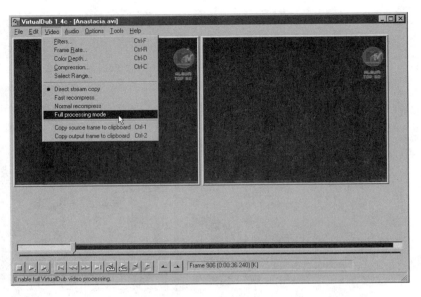

Under *Audio*, the *Full processing mode* must also be set.

Selecting the video codec

The desired video codec can be found under *Video/Compression...*

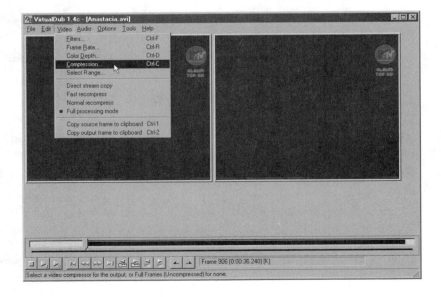

The list field behind it shows all available codecs.

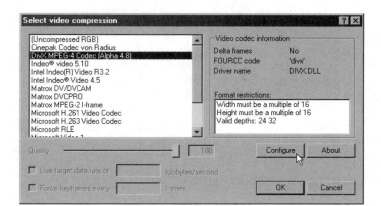

Clicking on an entry in *Format restrictions:* shows you the possible restrictions that must be considered.

Click the *Configure* button to adjust specific settings for each codec:

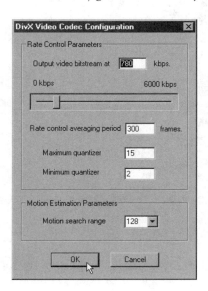

The desired data transfer rate can be set numerically or with the slider.

The value is KB/sec. For comparison: a video CD has a data transfer rate of 1100 kbps, a movie on DVD can reach rates of over 7000 kbps.

For this example, we will leave the default value of 780. The data transfer rate depends heavily on the image content.

It is advisable to capture the same video with different settings to recognize the strengths and weaknesses of the codec.

Now close the dialog box and return to the VirtualDub screen, to select the audio codec.

Selecting the audio codec

Here, select the menu option *Compression...*:

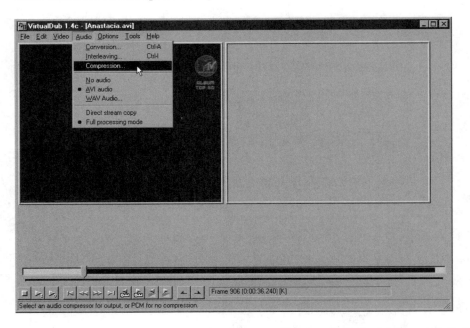

From the list, select the codec *DivX WMA Audio V2* supplied with OpenDivX. In the window to the right, you will see all data transfer rates available.

We will select the special video file preset of 64 KB (corresponding to 8 KB) per second:

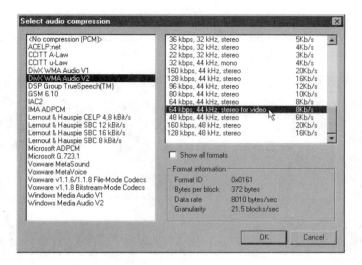

Saving the new video

Now all settings have been adjusted.

The video will now be created by going to *File/Save AVI...*:

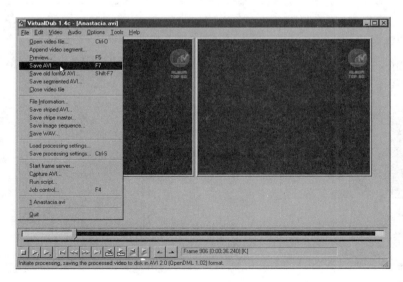

Select a name and storage location for the video clip.

Click on *OK* to start the process. The encoding process begins and can be followed as long as the options *Show input video* and *Show output video*, located in the lower part of the dialog window, are enabled.

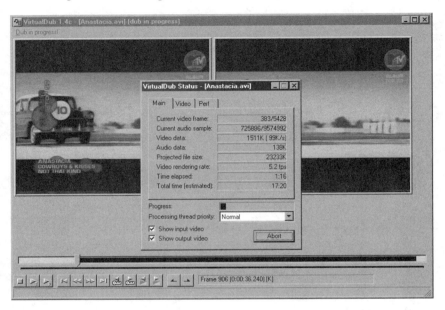

The dialog box informs you of the current video data transfer rate and the duration of the conversion process during the entire saving process.

The explorer box shows us the newly created video file compared to the original file:

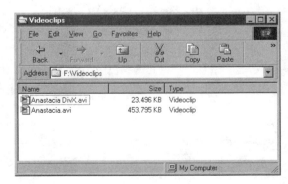

The size was reduced to a twentieth of the original.

2. From video camera or video recorder to PC

If you want to use your computer not only as a high-tech video recorder but also to process your movies, then you can make good use of VirtualDub.

If your graphics card or TV card has Video-in, you can connect it to a camcorder or video recorder as described on page 8.

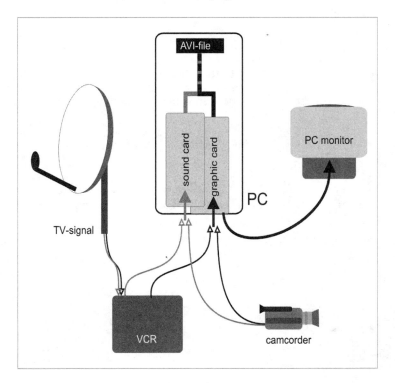

Obviously, those with a "real" video card can use the benefits of VirtualDub and need not use the capture tool supplied with the card.

It only has to be compatible with Video for Windows (also see page 22).

Unlike most TV cards, (analog) interface boards have hardware compression, i.e. the video signal is digitized through the chip in the card and needs only to be saved on the hard drive.

The advantage is that compression is not dependent on computer performance and videos can be captured with slower systems – even in full length.

2.1 Is everything connected?

Depending on the video hardware used, there are different sockets for video and audio signals.

All devices with line-out or S-video sockets such as Video-in are suitable as players.

Most audio line-outs are so-called Cinch sockets. If they are not there for some reason, you can always "misuse" the headphone socket as Audio-out.

You must have Video-in and Audio-in sockets available on the PC.

Some interface cards have built-in sound cards and have Video and Audio-in sockets, which is why they don't depend on external cards and don't cause compatibility problems.

There are also video cards like the DC10plus that are only concerned with the image signal. A separate sound card must be used for the audio signal.

Better cards with S-Video-in

Most recently, a PC card designed specifically for video interface offers another input, the S-video, Hosiden or Y/C socket:

If such sockets exist (one for in and one for out), they should be used, if possible, for the quality is visibly better thanks to separated color and brightness signals.

If these components have already been mixed, as with the simple composite signal (the corresponding sockets are often indicated with Line-In/Out), the image is visibly blurred.

Obviously, this inlet must have a corresponding outlet on the player. The simplest camcorders of the formats VHS-C or Video8 may not have such an S-video out, but all others have it, especially the new digital MiniDV or Digital8.

2.2 Is the image there?

If everything is connected as above, you should select the capture mode in VirtualDub by going to *File/Capture AVI...*, and display the current image, if the player is running.

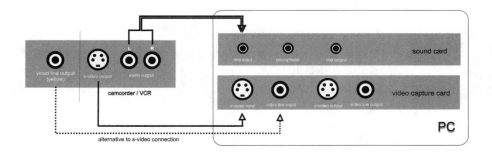

If this is not the case, then you should double-check two things:

1. **Have you selected the right capture drive?**

    If several cards that are related to the video are installed on the system, it may be that other capturing drivers are installed as well.

    In VirtualDub, it is easy to check this and to make the necessary changes.

    In the capture mode, go to *Video*. The available drivers are listed.

    Those activated have a dot before them.

    If you want to change a driver (and the card connected to it), select the new one simply by clicking on it.

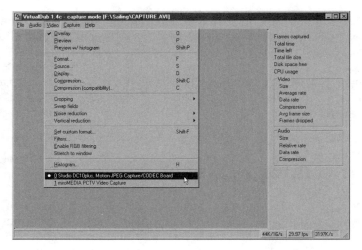

Here a TV card is installed in the PC, and its capture driver, *miroMEDIA PCTV Video Capture*, is activated.

2. Have you selected the correct Video-in?

Most often, a video card has two different in channels, namely the Line and S-video sockets.

If the camcorder is connected to the S-video-in of the video card, this must also be selected in the driver software of the card.

With VirtualDub, you can access the relevant driver by going to *Video/Source* in the menu.

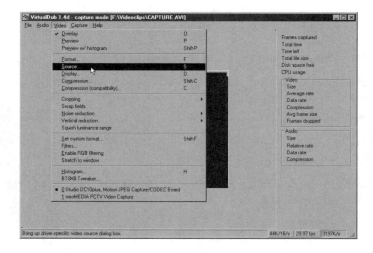

Now call up the video card interface (it will have a different appearance from model to model and version to version).

The following image appears with DC10plus:

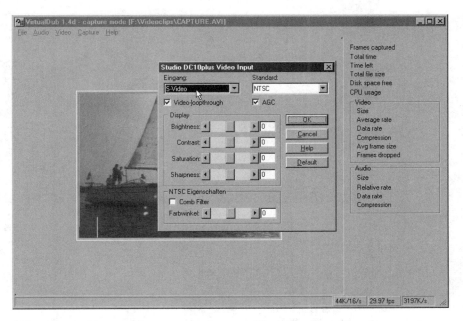

Selecting S-video as the current Input will make the video image appear immediately on the screen.

In addition to this function, the hardware can also influence the image quality regarding brightness, contrast and color saturation and sharpness, enabling the video to be captured as best as possible.

2.3 Selecting the interface card format

When you're choosing the format and the compression in VirtualDub, the differences between the models become evident:

For example, if you own the Pinnacle DC10plus and select the menu option *Vide/Format* ...

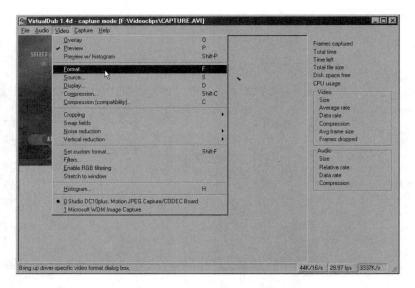

... you directly access the internal interface. Here, you can determine all image parameters for the capture:

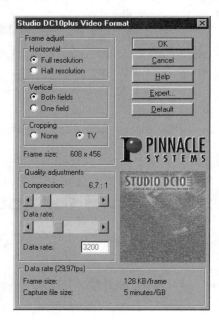

In the upper area, you can achieve different quality levels by combining various horizontal and vertical (here: "temporal") resolution settings. This facilitates the adaptation to the system's performance.

The smallest resolution is given by combining *Half Resolution* with *One Field*, which corresponds to the usual quarter screen resolution for TV cards (360 x 270 pixels):

For maximum quality, you should record both fields in full horizontal resolution:

If *Cropping None* is selected simultaneously, the full NTSC format of 720 x 540 pixels can be used:

Because the full image is not displayed on the TV screen anyway, you can do away with the area that is not visible and thus save space when recording.

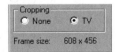

For each image format, a data transfer rate can be set with the slider:

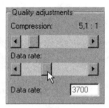

The higher the value selected, the less the video has to be compressed, which leads to better capturing quality. The amount of space needed does increase, however.

With this card, a special information field informs you of the amount of memory used by the current settings, thus it is possible to use the available space to the fullest:

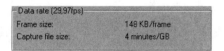

Increasing the data transfer rate places high demands on the hard drive, because large amounts of data have to be written without interruption, so there are no jerks or data losses. You can determine whether the data transfer rate is realistic by using the test routine in VirtualDub.

2.4 Expanding the formats with *Custom format*

In some cases, selecting a specific format can be beneficial.

If you want to create a video CD from the captured material, for example, it is best to use the CD format (352 x 240 pixels) or an exact multiple of it for the capturing, because it ensures the best result for the subsequent MPEG encoding.

The capture board DC10plus shown here does not have these pixel ratios available.

VirtualDub offers the option of setting your own format with the menu option *Video/Set custom format...*:

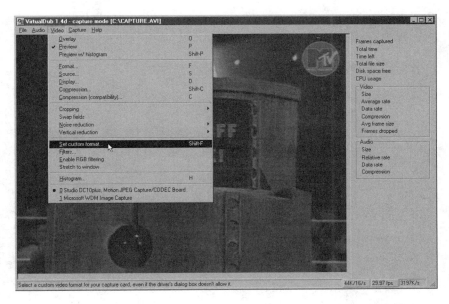

In this way, you can make the video card also capture in formats previously alien to it:

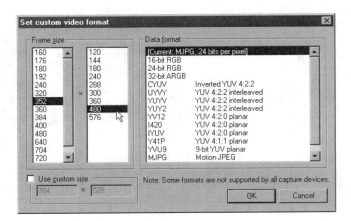

The list of different color formats on the right has little significance for most video capture cards, as they use their own formats and do not accept others.

Although selection seems possible at first, an error message appears when you start capturing:

The internal change is not visible in the video image ...

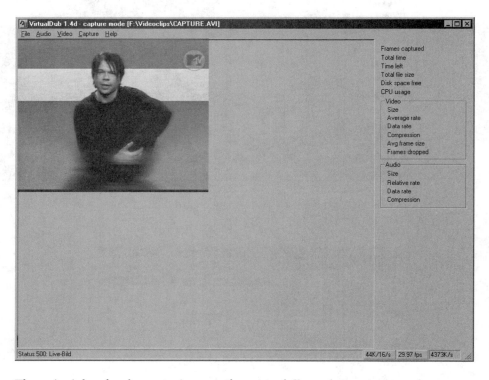

The principle of only capturing one frame in full resolution is a good compromise between image size and quality, particularly when capturing is only an intermediate stage in creating the file. All additional image information will contribute to a better result when you convert the file to the desired format.

2.5 Selecting the compression with video capture cards

Many analog video capture cards capture in the MJPEG ("Motion JPEG") format and rely on a codec produced by the manufacturer and installed at the same time as the driver.

For this reason, the dialog boxes *Video/Compression...* or *Video/Compression (compatibility)...* offers no alternative compression:

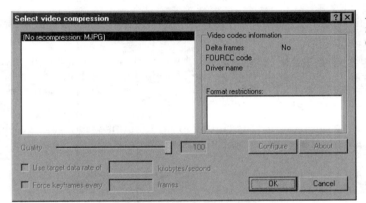

Dialog box for the menu option Video/ Compression

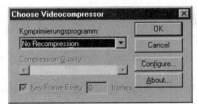

Dialog box for the menu option Video/Compression (compatibility)

2.6 Specific problems for cards with Zoran chip sets

Motion-JPEG based cards, whose hardware is based on Zoran chip sets (including DC10plus) cause problems for VirtualDub, if the internal capture mode is used. Data transfer rates are not adhered to, which causes *Dropped frames*.

No problems may occur in the compatibility mode. In the meantime, almost every capture card has corresponding software which is able to circumvent file size limitations (see page 45), so VirtualDub does not have to be used for such tasks.

2.7 Capturing tips

When all settings have been made, you can now capture videos onto the hard drive.

Depending on your plans, following some tips can make the process easier for you.

1. If the video file is to be processed further in an editing program like Movie-Xone, it is advised to digitize the material block by block or scene by scene. This provides more of an overview, so that you are not searching endlessly for certain sections of a clip.

2. Create a directory for the editing project. In this way it can be deleted easily after use without harming other files.

Now you can capture the video clip. This is described in depth starting on page 41. This is only a brief description:

1. Start VirtualDub in the capture mode (*File/Capture AVI...*)

2. Create a project directory on the hard drive (e. g. *Sailing*) and enter the capture files into it with *File/Set capture file...*

3. Start the internal mode capture with *Capture/Capture video...* (F6). Alternatively, you can use the compatibility mode by going to *Capture/Capture video (compatibility mode)* (F5) (more detail about this process on page 41).

4. Rename the file *capture.avi* according to its content. You can now begin a new capturing process.

2.8 Super 8 movies on the PC?

Before you process the video material with an editing program, we should look at a type of amateur movie we have not addressed before, namely the Super 8 movie.

Long before the home video era, family memories were captured on proper film material, mostly in normal and Super 8 formats known as "cinefilm".

Such movies probably still exist in quite a few homes, but are rarely viewed owing to the hassle of setting up a projector and screen. Besides, they often have no sound.

A modern medium like digital video – whether on tape or (video) CD – is a good way of editing such treasures in order to bring them to new life (maybe by adding sound) on the big-screen TV.

Transferring Super 8 to video

To get Super 8 movies into the computer, you need the intermediate "video tape" stage. Further processing occurs with a suitable TV or video card, as already described in chapter 2.

If the movie has to be transferred onto video cassette, there are two ways of doing this:

Professional transfer

There are companies that can transfer cinefilm onto very high quality video.

Depending on the process, such movie scanning can cost between $ 1.50 and $ 2.50 per minute of movie material. The more expensive processes are wet-gate processes in which the film is run through a fluid to eliminate dust and scratches almost entirely.

In any case, we advise a digital video system like MiniDV as the end format. In this way, you can make an identical copy of the expensive original at any time and can edit it without losses on the computer.

Do-it-yourself transfer by filming with a camcorder

Those who want to avoid the cost of professional transfer and who have a camcorder can transfer movies to video on their own – just not in the same quality as modern scanners.

Depending on the quality and equipment of the projector, you can nevertheless make respectable copies.

An example of a simple system:

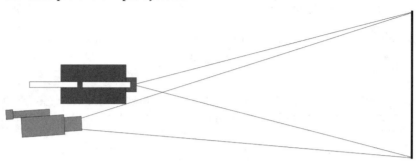

The projection should occur in a very dark room. A matte white screen with no surface structure is the most suitable projection surface.

The camera must be as close as possible to the visual axis of the movie projector in order to control image distortions and sharpness.

Technical tips:

- The camera should be firmly fixed on a tripod, and the focus set manually, if possible (otherwise it might auto focus).

- The camcorder's aperture should be set manually. You can determine the approximate aperture in a few trials. Owing to the considerably high contrast of the film material, you may have to adjust the aperture for different scenes during filming.

- Allow the white balance to be set automatically.

- It is more difficult to eliminate flickering caused by different frame rates (film: 18 or 24 frames/sec, video: 25 frames/sec). Deluxe projectors like those from Beaulieu have adjustable sector shutters which allow the individual frames to be illuminated longer, thus reducing flickering. Another option is to extend the shutter speed to 1/25 second ("slow shutter"). Check your camera manual to see whether this is possible. If you don't have any of these refinements at your disposal, you may have to resort to changing the projection speed (try to do so as smoothly as possible) – a feature built into many projectors.

3. Processing the video material

When capture is complete, you can begin editing the material with any editor, whereby VirtualDub only acts as a capture tool. But the program can do much more:

The captured video and audio files can be filtered and converted into other formats.

3.1 Using the options of VirtualDub

You can optimize the video material for editing with VirtualDub as the "video processor".

Proceed in the following manner:

1   Open a clip.

2   Modify the clip by allocating filters and possibly new in and out points.

3   Export the result as a new clip.

If you were still bound to the driver and graphics/TV/video interface codecs while capturing, you can output in any file format (provided the corresponding codec is installed).

A filter interface for editing video clips is integrated into VirtualDub. With its help, you can undertake a vast number of corrections and defamiliarizations in a very simple manner.

In the following example, we would like to process a clip with a filter and convert it into a space-saving format.

In addition to the integrated filters, you can download others from the Internet and add them to VirtualDub. You can find a link to other filters at http://www.virtualdub.org.

Installing additional filters

Such additional filters are very small files and can be downloaded in a relatively short space of time.

In order for VirtualDub to recognize a filter the next time the program starts, you need only copy/move the file into the plug-in directory (with the extension *.vcf):

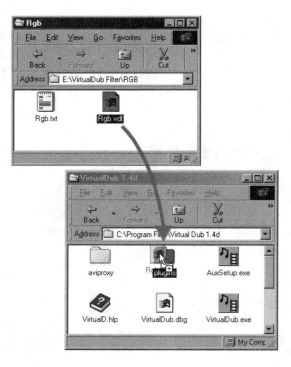

Assigning video filters

When VirtualDub is started again, you can assign one or more filters to an opened clip as follows.

By using an RGB filter you can carry out color corrections:

1 Go to *Video/Filters...*

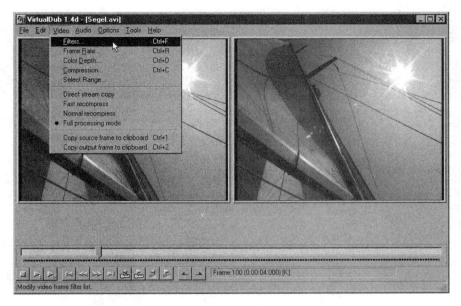

The window that appears is empty. It will later list all the filters you have used.

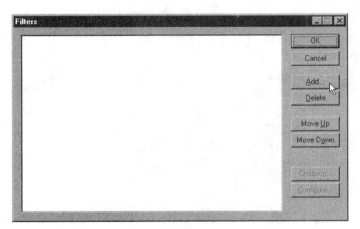

2 Click on the *Add...* button, and all available filters are shown (you can find the most important filters and their effects on page 89):

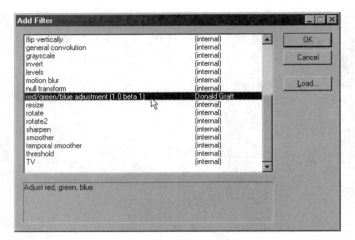

3 Select the filter and confirm with OK.

4 In the subsequent dialog box, click on *Show Preview* to check the changes directly on the video image:

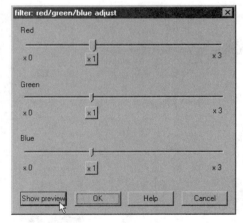

5 Now you can adjust the values for the primary colors *Red*, *Green* and *Blue* with the sliders:

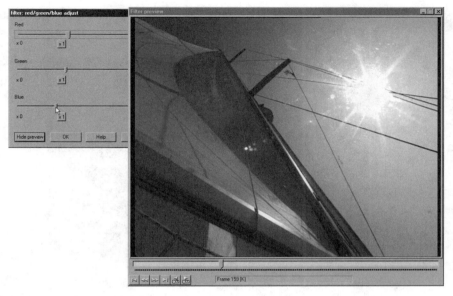

6 Clicking OK takes you back to the list, to which the *red/green/blue adjustment* has just been added:

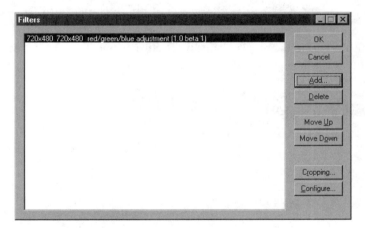

Any number of filters can be added in this way.

You leave the filter menu by clicking on *OK*.

When you are in the main window again, you can assess the result in the monitor window on the right:

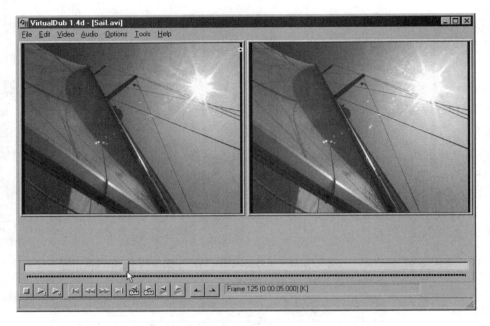

Click on the relevant play button (O) to run most filters in real time (even if more than one is activated):

Filter overview

VirtualDub has a lot of integrated filters.

Here are all internal filters and their functions:

Filter name	Function	Preview
2:1 reduction (high quality)	Reduces the image by halving the width and height to a quarter of the screen area.	No
3x3 average	Each pixel is made from the average of the pixels surrounding it. Causes slight blurring.	No
blur	Creates a slight blur that is almost imperceptible in a full picture.	No
blur more	Stronger blurring.	No
box blur	Blurring can be defined	Yes
brightness/contrast	Brightness and contrast control	No
deinterlace	Joins half frames together.	No
emboss	Effect filter: image shown as relief (can be set).	No
field swap	Swaps the half frame sequence.	No
fill	A rectangle can be set and filled with the desired color.	Yes
flip horizontally / flip vertically	Flips a frame horizontally or vertically.	No
general convolution	Type of image processor that affects each pixel according to its color, as well as those surrounding it. Some values have to be entered into a matrix.	No
grayscale	Changes video clips to black and white.	No
invert	Inverts the colors into a "negative".	No
motion blur	Creates a type of motion blur by "resonating" the previous images.	No
resize	Image format can be set with pixel accuracy.	Yes
rotate	The video image can be rotated in 90° steps. Pixel measurements can be changed this way as well.	No
rotate2	Rotates the image by any angle.	Yes
sharpen	Increases the contrast of the edges to sharpen the image (can be set).	No
smoother	A dynamic soft focus that tries to retain edges and contours. Can reduce distortion.	Yes
temporal smoother	Like motion blur but constantly increasing.	Yes
threshold	Converts the image to pure black and white. The threshold can be set.	No
TV	Converts the image to NTSC.	No

3.2 VirtualDub and its limits

If you want to process your digital recordings even further and insert titles, create certain transitions between individual frames, or insert/dub audio, then VirtualDub alone cannot help you, and you will need an appropriate video editing program.

If you think that such a program will cost a small fortune, then you are wrong.

One such application is MovieXone from Aist Medialab Inc. This program can be installed from the included CD-ROM.

You can find further information about MovieXone and a downloading possibility at *www.aist.com*.

3.3 Post-production with MovieXone

MovieXone is a proper video editing program, which is similar in use to other big programs.

With it, you can combine clips into a movie, make small corrections to individual scenes and add titles. You can also add a soundtrack or spoken commentary.

The finished product can be published in many ways: for instance, it can be sent out as an e-mail or burned onto a video CD.

Installation

The software almost installs itself. Once you have accepted the licensing conditions, you must decide in which directory to copy the program files.

The following question appears during the procedure:

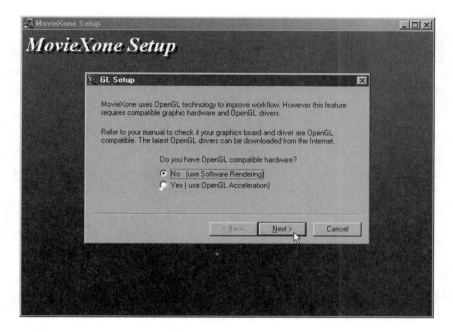

The dialog box is almost self-explanatory.

Here you must state whether a graphics card that supports MovieXone Open-GL acceleration is installed.

If you are unsure, select No and use the slower software support.

After restarting the computer, a shortcut icon for MovieXone is placed on the desktop.

MovieXone

The basic settings when starting the program

Each time the program starts, the video standard (NTSC for the US) is established.

An editing project in MovieXone is called an *Animation*.

Here you can define the basic profile of the prospective animation.

Under *Schemes*, you will find the current settings. These can be adjusted in the neighboring tabs:

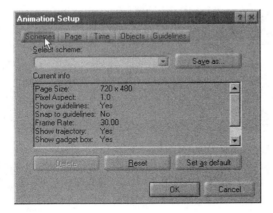

Should you change these values in any way, you can save them here as the new scheme.

In the *Page* tab, you can define the video page proportions for your project. Ideally, all clips that you want to process for your movie have the same format, i.e. they were digitalized with the same settings.

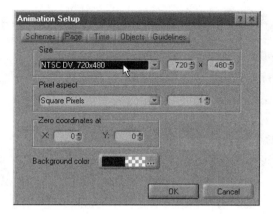

720 x 480 pixels is the typical NTSC format which is used by many analog video cards and the now widespread digital DV format.

To the right of the *Time* tab, in which you selected the video format in the beginning, there are two further tabs available, which only give you some more viewing options. For the sake of completeness, we will present them as well.

In the *Objects* tab, you can determine the viewing options for objects in the animation window.

Any clip or text can be an object and can be placed anywhere in the animation window, as we will demonstrate with a text in the following (see page 116).

If such an object is duplicated, you can create an offset by adjusting the numbers in the *Duplicate shift* area, so that the copy does not lie exactly on the original and can be accessed more easily.

(Such duplicates cannot be created with the freeware version of MovieXone, because it supports only compositing.)

Checkmark the *Show Gadget Box* option, if you want to give the object a frame. Select the color of the frame from the *Gadget color* palette.

If an object is to move in the movie, the motion is displayed as a trajectory – provided that the *Show Trajectory* option has been activated.

Once everything is activated, display begins, as with our text object on page 117.

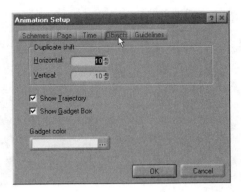

In the last part of the animation settings, you can define guidelines which can help with the exact positioning of the object.

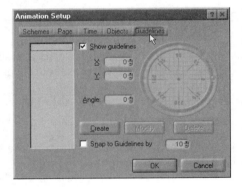

More practical guidelines can also be taken from the animation window at any time:

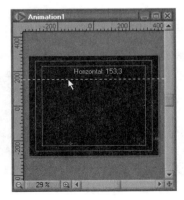

The basic structure of MovieXone

When you close the dialog box, you have adjusted all the significant settings, and the basic configuration screen of MovieXone appears:

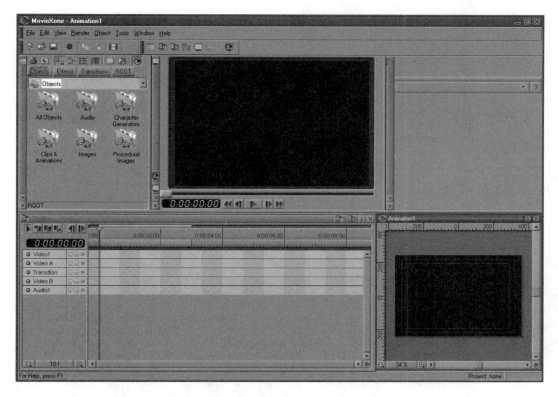

Basically, the window is split into three areas which we will briefly introduce at this point:

1. The browser

If you want to edit a movie, you need raw material like individual video clips, graphics, sounds, but also dissolves.

With the browser, you can access these individual components quickly:

This is a lot like Explorer; thus, you can access directories by double-clicking on them.

2. The timeline

The timeline is the area where our movie is created. Here, all components are brought together and placed in a chronological sequence.

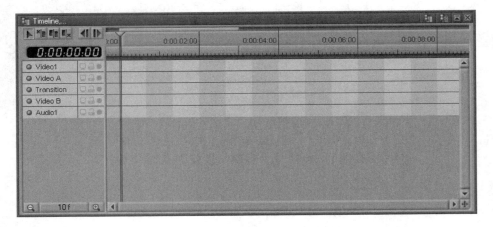

Over the years, a certain system has materialized that is used in all video editing programs:

The timeline, which is displayed as a kind of ruler at the top of the screen, progresses from left to right.

The video tracks run in the same direction one under the other. Underneath run the corresponding sound tracks. Image and sound are represented separately, which facilitates access to the components of a movie clip.

To view a specific part of a movie, use the so-called timeslider in the form of a blue line. You can drag the line over the timeline and drop it at the desired point:

The movie scene selected above can then be seen in the following window.

3. The preview screen

This window represents a virtual studio window and shows exactly the image selected with the timeslider. You can control it with the control buttons at the bottom.

First steps: browsing the video material

As mentioned before, the browser is the interface used by MovieXone to access the necessary material.

If you have digitized the movie scenes in their own directory, this pays off now.

In only a few steps, you can place the clips in their own tab:

1 Click on the *Add tab* icon to create a new tab.

A new tab is always located in the root directory.

2 Double-click on *Movie*.

The desktop appears as in Windows Explorer.

3 Open it by double-clicking on it, and select the directory containing the video files from the available drives.

There, all clips are shown as thumbnails.

Trimming individual clips

The clips in the directory are in their digitized state, of course. Should you only want to use a section of such a file, you need to determine new starting and ending points. Experts call this "trimming".

The clip is not changed in any way, as MovieXone remembers only the section to be played back. Trimming a video clip is simple:

1 If you keep the mouse over a clip for a while, a preview is launched in a small window.

2 With the slider, find the position in this clip that you want to appear in your movie. For exact control use the buttons to the left and right of the play button.

3 Set a new start tag by clicking on *IN*.

The area of the clip that will be visible later (marked in blue) is instantly shortened.

4 The end tag is determined in the same way. Click on "Out" to set it.

You can trim all clips to the desired length in this manner. Changes can be made at any time, of course.

Arranging clips on the timeline

The actual movie is created by arranging the different clips on the timeline.

There are two options for executing this, and it is up to you to choose the best method for you.

a) Inserting clips from the viewer

The viewing window is not only suitable for trimming clips.

The clips viewed there can be sent to the timeline at the touch of a button:

1   Select the track to which you want to export the clip.

On the left side of the timeline window there is a button like a small light that you click once.

2   Set the timeslider to the position where the clip should start (here no clip is set, and the slider is at 0:00:00:00).

Should there already be a clip at that position on the selected track, the new clip is placed on the next higher track.

3   Roll the mouse over the icon of the clip to be added to open the playback window. Click on *INS* ...

... to reset the scene to 0:00:00:00 on the Video A track:

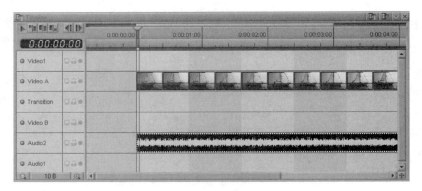

b) Dragging clips onto the timeline (drag and drop)

Another way of bringing a clip to the timeline is to click on it with the mouse and to drag it to the relevant position on the timeline while holding the mouse button down.

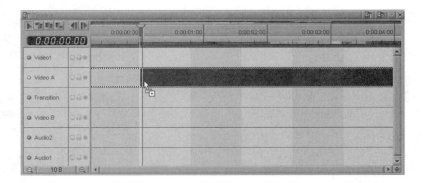

As long as the mouse button is not released, the dark area representing the clip can be shifted as desired.

Different insertion methods

If you hold down the Shift key during the drag & drop process, after dropping, a window appears where you can select an insertion method:

Insert is best for inserting a clip between two already existing ones.

With *Cut & Insert*, you can slice a clip already on the timeline along the insert position, and push the second half backwards by the length of the inserted clip.

Place facilitates inserting a clip into a gap provided it is big enough.

With *Connect*, you can attach a clip to a movie that already exists without having to place it in an exact position. You only have to "hit" the last clip in the movie.

With *Replace*, the clip overwrites everything on the track within the clip's dimensions.

New track dispatches the clip onto a new track. The freeware version of MovieXone has its restrictions, however, and enables only a compositing track (the existing Video1). Choosing this command can call up a warning message

With *Fill*, you can fill a gap on the track, whereby the scene to be inserted can be placed on top of the clip before the gap. If the scene is bigger than the gap, the clip is trimmed accordingly.

Modify decides how the insertion method will affect the subsequent clips/track:

Current track shifts only the scenes on the track into which the clip is to be inserted.

Current group shifts only objects on the compositing tracks.

All shifts all the clips on all the tracks.

Different display modes for the timeline and clips

In the example above, the clip inserted into the timeline runs off the screen.

In order to not lose the overview, you can reduce the display. Zoom in to work on image details.

This is carried out with the zoom buttons in the left-hand corner below the timeline. The number between them shows the current zoom factor. Where you once saw 10 individual frames of a film clip, now you can only see one.

Zooming back out to *5 sec* allows you to view the whole dimension of the inserted clip.

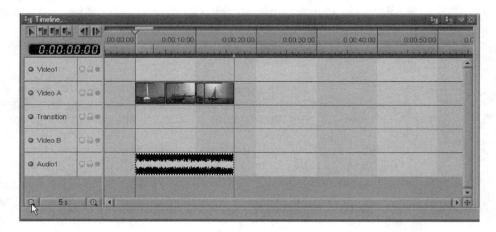

If a video scene is placed on the timeline, it can be displayed in different ways.

The display mode selected here is the most time-consuming but also the most exact, for the clip is displayed as individual frames throughout, which can result in a longer lasting picture composition when you have a lot of clips on the timeline.

Right-click on the timeline to open a context-sensitive menu. Choose the last entry, *Timeline Setup...*:

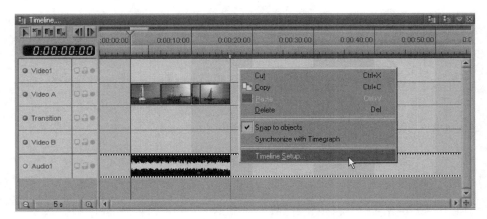

In the dialog box that opens, you can determine the display of the clips on the timeline:

The track format *First and Last* is a tried and proven one. The clip is easily recognizable from the content; in addition, its name is shown between the start and end of the image.

The preview area

Important: only where a preview area is set (green bar below the timeline) can the relevant spot be displayed in the preview area.

The size of this area can – as with clips – be altered by dragging the margins. The area can also be shifted.

If the preview area cannot be manipulated, it can be created again by pressing the Ctrl key and clicking with the mouse.

Other important options in the timeline

To put the scenes together into a movie, you need to place them in chronological order, as already described.

Moving clips with the hand

Everywhere where there is no clip, the cursor becomes a hand, with which you can shift the entire timeline by keeping the mouse button depressed. This way, you can quickly find any position:

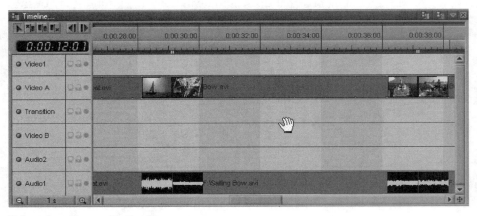

Trimming clips on the timeline

If you have already dragged scenes onto the tracks, you may find out that they need to be further shortened or elongated.

To shorten a clip located in the middle of a sequence, proceed as follows:

1 Holding down the Alt key simultaneously with the mouse button makes the cursor appear as shown. When this occurs, you can move the starting point of the clip to the left:

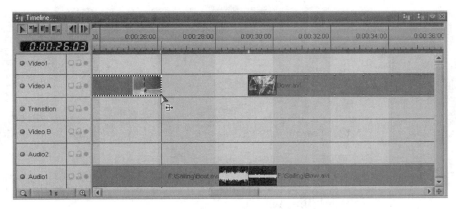

In doing so, you don't "compress" the clip and don't make it play faster – it just ends earlier.

2 The same can be done with the corresponding soundtrack (you do not need to press Alt here):

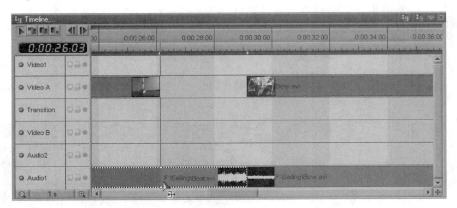

On reaching the starting point of the clip, the mouse gently locks into place, which allows you to make the audio clip of the exact same length as the video clip.

3 Now all following clips have to be shifted up to the altered clip.

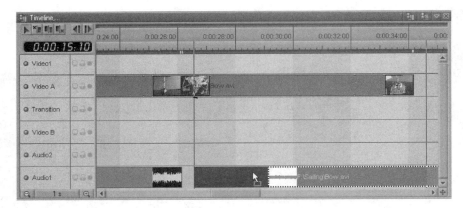

Important: Ensure that the video and sound components aren't coupled in MovieXone, and that they must be moved separately. Also, ensure that you carry out the same steps with both components of a clip, so that sound and image remain in synch.

Inserting dissolves

99% of movies are made with two types of cuts. In addition to letting scene follow upon scene (hard cut), there is also the possibility of slowly "dissolving" one scene into the next (soft cut).

Such dissolves can be created quickly:

1 The first clip is on the Video A track. Move the second clip on the Video B track ...

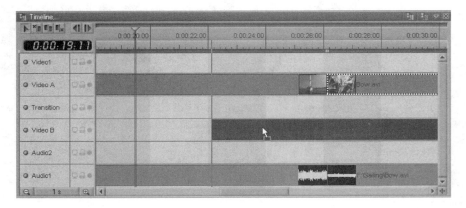

... so that they overlap by a certain amount:

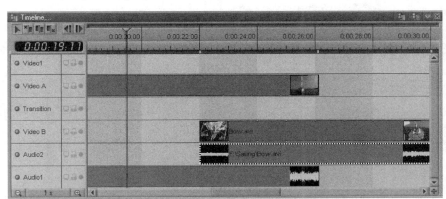

2 In the browser, select *Transitions* in any one of the tabs.

3 Now double-click on *All Transitions*.

4 In this directory, you will find only the standard *Dissolve* which you can use like a clip.

Drag the dissolve between the two relevant clips.

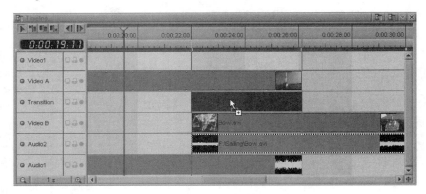

5 Spot check the dissolve with the help of the timeslider.

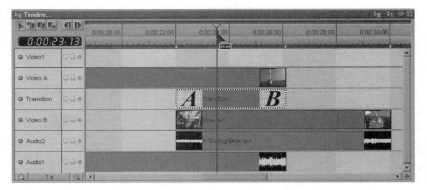

You can view the results in the neighboring window:

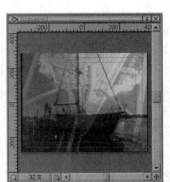

Is it dissolving the wrong way?

If such a dissolve is used, MovieXone automatically attempts to set the right direction.

If the dissolve runs in the wrong direction for some reason, i.e. if you have a hard cut, the second scene dissolves into the first, and, finally, another hard cut takes you to the second scene, the direction of the dissolve must be reversed as follows:

1 Select the relevant dissolve.

2 Place the timeslider in the dissolve area.

3 The parameters of the dissolve appear in the *Effect box*. Set the option *Exchange A and B Sources* to *On* ...

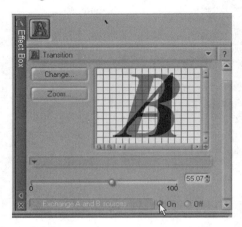

... and the dissolve runs in the opposite direction.

Creating fade ins and fade outs

With *Dissolve* you can also easily create fade ins and fade outs. This involves fading from a scene to black (not to another clip) and vice versa.

With this technique you can start or end movies.

Text in movies

A real movie needs a title.

With MovieXone, you can insert a one-line text into a running image.

Search the browser for the *Character Generators* directory and double-click on it:

Click on the object *Text string* ...

... and drag it onto the timeline:

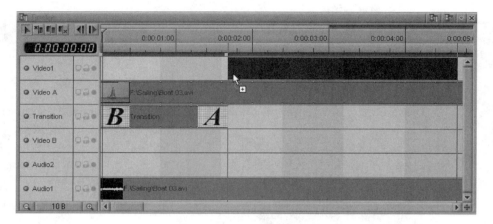

In our example, we want the movie to begin with a fade in and the title to appear immediately behind it.

Go with the timeslider to the text clip area to immediately see the result on the preview screen:

"MoviePack" is a preset text that can be edited in the lower portion of the effect box when the text clip is active and the timeslider is located on it:

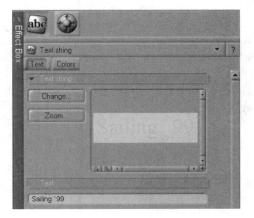

Scroll down the effect box window to reach the *Font...* button and choose a different font:

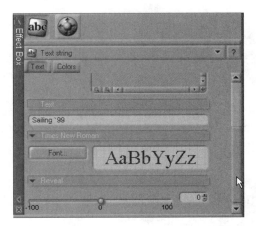

The size of the title is defined in the animation window. MovieXone can recognize the parameters of an object at any time during the movie.

We want to elucidate this with the help of a simple example:

Let's assume that the title should move from left to right across the image. In this case, we only need to define a starting and ending point in the animation window. MovieXone calculates the intermediate steps.

Moving titles in movies with key frames

1 Place the slide ruler to the beginning of the title clip.

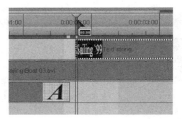

2 In the animation window, set the starting size and position with the mouse. Drag one of the edges to resize the text.

3 Zoom out with the buttons in the bottom left corner of the animation window in order to see a larger area outside of the movie window. Click in the middle of the text and drag it out of the picture by holding down the mouse button:

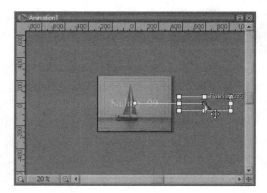

4 Position the timeslider in the timeline to the end of the title clip.

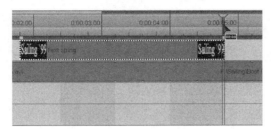

5 Repeat steps 2 and 3, so that the animation window looks like this:

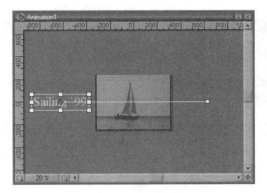

6 By clicking along the title clip, you can see how the text travels across the image.

Rendering the finished movie

Once the work is finished and the completed movie is on the timeline, you may ask yourself what happens now.

Like VirtualDub, MovieXone can export the movie in different formats.

Exporting is called *Rendering* and can be applied to the whole timeline or to a defined section of it.

In MovieXone, this function is launched by going to *Render/Render*:

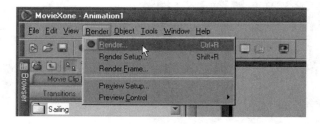

A file selection box appears that allows you to name the video file:

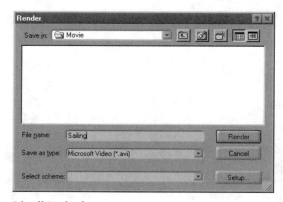

It's all in the format

You can decide the format of the file by clicking on *Setup...*

A dialog box with four tabs appears. You can adjust all the necessary settings here.

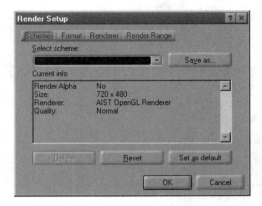

In the *Schemes* tab, you can name and save the set profile, which allows you to quickly activate it for future exports in the same format.

In the following tabs such settings can be made as accurately as possible.

Let us begin with the format-independent settings, like the *Render Range*.

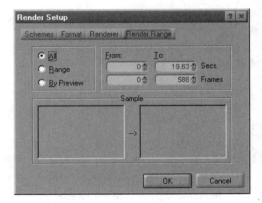

You can render either the whole movie (*All*) or only a section of it (*Range*). The values in *From* and *To* correspond to the range defined in the timeline and are indicated by an orange line. To define the range, click with your mouse while holding down the Ctrl key. You can then extend or shift it like a clip:

In the *Renderer* tab, you can select the internal renderer and the quality level:

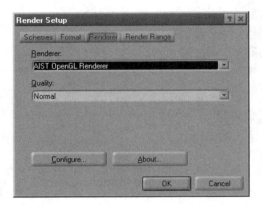

The decisive settings for the rendering can be found in the *Format* tab.

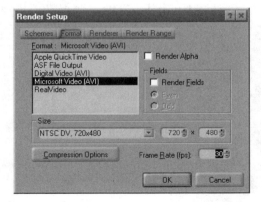

Depending on the purpose, different formats can be selected:

- **Digital video**

    MovieXone supports direct video in and video export for digital video formats like MiniDV or Digital8, as long as the PC has an appropriate interface, usually an expansion card.

Such cards have several designations, but they mean the same thing: IEEE-1394, Firewire or i-Link from Sony stand for a small connection which enables the simultaneous transfer of image and sound data from the camcorder to the computer hard drives over a single cable. If the camcorder has another DV-in, it can even be used as a recorder for the finished movie.

If this format is to be created, select *Digital Video (AVI)*:

- **Analog formats of TV/video cards for transfer to video tape**

If analog sources are to be digitized with a TV or video card (either via VirtualDub, MovieXone or the recording software in the video card), it is advised that the finished movie is saved in the same format as the original clips and played back with the video card software in order to record it onto video over the analog outlets.

Here the individual clips were digitized with the MJPEG codec of DC10plus.

To launch the codecs installed in Windows, select *Microsoft Video (AVI)*:

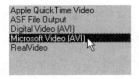

The image size should be that of the original material – here *720x480*:

With *Compression Options* you can select the codec:

Under *Video Compression*, you can select the video card codec from the pull-down menu:

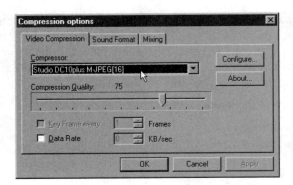

Depending on the codec, this dialog box has different parameter settings (here, for instance, the compression quality can be set with a slider).

All other settings should be left as they are.

Exporting for (Super) video CD

In order for the movie to be burned onto a CD and be played back by a DVD player, it must be converted to the MPEG-1 or MPEG-2 format, which is not possible in MovieXone but only with a special encoder program like TMPEGEnc (included on the CD).

As before, the same codec used for capturing the clip must be used to export it, in order to avoid data loss. The higher the quality of the original material in TMPEGEnc, the better the MPEG files will be.

You will find a description of creating video or Super video CDs in chapter 7.

Exporting as an Internet movie

If the finished movie is to appear on a website, it has to fulfill certain requirements. Given the current technical possibilities, you have to make definite cuts to the image size and data rate.

Clearly, the most well-known and widespread formats are ASF, developed by Microsoft, and Realvideo from Real Networks, which are both supported by MovieXone.

These formats are so-called streaming formats, meaning that such movies do not have to be downloaded before playing but are played during download. If the data connection is slow, there can be breaks in the movie until more data has been downloaded.

Creating such video streams is very easy with MovieXone.

1 Select the *Format* (here *RealVideo*).

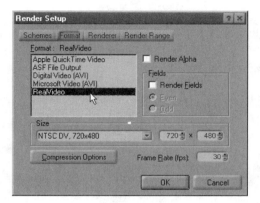

2 For the image size, use smaller dimensions, like 160 x 120 pixels:

3 Usually, a frame rate of 15 frames/sec is fast enough.

Once the *Frame Rate* is set, go to *Compression Options...*

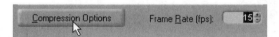

4 Here, you can adjust the quality and size settings for the RealVideo file.

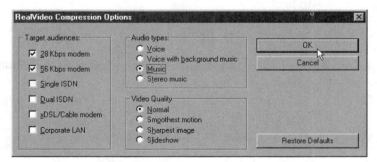

The *Target audience* should be the owners of 56KB modems or higher. A lower transfer rate would not achieve acceptable results.

Under *Audio types*, select the sound to be used. However: the higher the sound quality, the less space there is for image quality. Simply test different settings to get an idea of the video created (you will need the corresponding RealPlayer for playback).

Finally, you can decide, whether the *Smoothest motion* or the *Sharpest image* is more important to you. *Normal* is a compromise, while *Slideshow* refers to static images appearing in sequence.

The actual rendering process

If all format settings have been adjusted, you can close the dialog box and return to the file selection box.

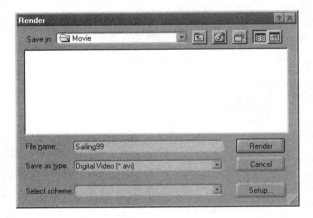

Once the name of the movie file is entered, you can start the rendering process by clicking on *Render*.

You can follow the entire procedure in a special window.

Click on the *Preview* button to extend the window in order to follow the current status and recognize possible errors.

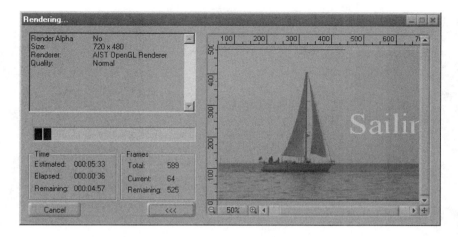

If the same format as that of the original material is selected for the movie, only the amended sections, like dissolves or title insertions, have to be rendered. Unchanged sections are only copied, which can speed up the rendering process.

Unless rendering has been interrupted by clicking on *Cancel*, the following message appears after a successful rendering:

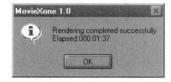

3. Processing the video material

4. From DVD to PC

If you have ever tried to copy a DVD movie file from your DVD-Rom onto your hard drive, you will have probably encountered the following message:

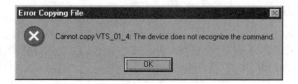

The reason for this is that DVDs are usually copy protected to prevent such copying.

Because copy protections are created by mere humans, it was only a matter of time until someone found a way around this one, and so, a "remedy" was born in Norway in the form of a small program.

The software named DeCSS ("De-Content Scrambling System") cracks the DVD encryption and facilitates copying files onto the hard drive. The first versions of DeCSS were difficult to use, but more convenient versions have since appeared to facilitate such copying.

Important: this process – known as "ripping" – is completely prohibited and thus illegal unless the DVDs belong to you, or unless you have obtained express permission to make a copy.

If you search for such tools on the Internet, you will sooner or later stumble upon "SmartRipper", which allows you to copy entire DVDs or a specific section of them onto your hard drive.

4.1 Collecting trailers on CD

Many DVDs contain trailers (which appear in cinemas before a movie is released) in addition to the main feature.

These trailers are spread over many of your DVDs, and it would be great to put them onto one CD to enjoy them in sequence.

The legal consequences must be stressed again: in essence, you will be making pirated copies of these trailers, which is punishable by law.

Copying trailer files onto the hard drive with SmartRipper

With SmartRipper, you can access the desired trailer and copy it into the directory of your choice on your PC, provided your PC has a DVD-ROM drive (a normal CD-ROM drive cannot read DVDs).

Place the DVD in the drive and start your DVD player software, such as PowerDVD.

If the DVD is recognized and played back, you can close the player and launch SmartRipper. With many films, this process first decrypts the data and helps if the ripping procedure (see page 135) does not start.

The DVD is analyzed and read:

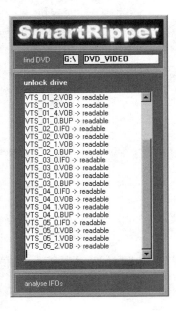

Now, the main window of the program launches.

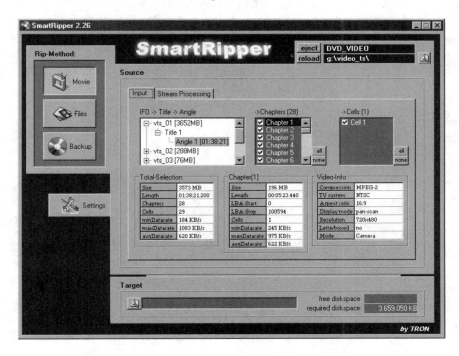

There are essentially three copying modes in SmartRipper that can be selected by clicking on the buttons on the left:

In *Movie* mode, with which we will deal in detail shortly, whole sections of movies can be copied.

Clicking on *Files* enables the transfer of selected files onto the hard drive:

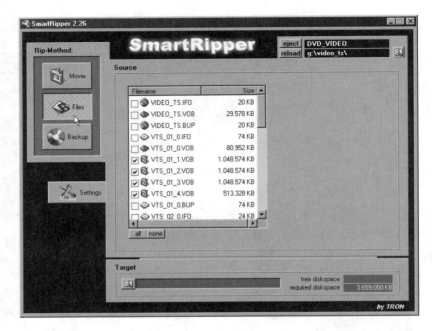

In *Backup* mode, you can make a backup copy of your DVD on your PC:

Let us return to the most interesting setting: *Movie*.

In its main window, a plethora of information is shown after the DVD has been read:

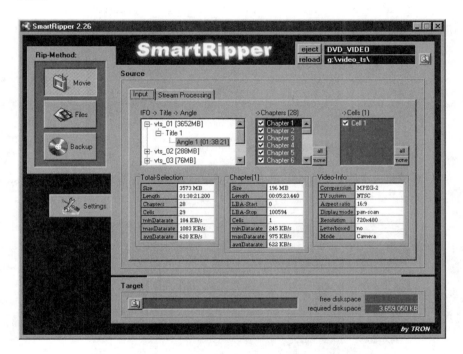

At the top of the program window, you will find information concerning the composition of a selected track on the DVD.

The content of this window is obviously different from disc to disc.

In the window on the left, the hierarchically unfolding content of the IFO files (IFO=Information) is shown.

This is simply a table of contents for the data that is actually saved in the VOB-files (VOB=Video Objects) of a DVD.

The IFOs list the titles located in them – usually movie excerpts – but also navigation menus, etc. These titles can consist of several *Angles*, but that would be the exception.

In this case, the main movie on the DVD (duration 1 hour, 38 minutes and 21 seconds) was specifically chosen using the mouse.

Details concerning the title selected in the window on the left will be shown in the neighboring window.

In our example, the movie consists of 28 chapters.

Click on the *Stream Processing* tab and check *Enable* to display the exact content of the selected track.

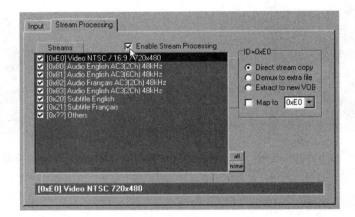

Here, the underlying versions, such as variations in language and subtitles, are displayed to a certain extent.

The movie exists in an English and French version, all in AC3 format (the old term for Dolby Digital).

The merits of software like SmartRipper is that it can display the information contained in these VOB files as desired and, depending on the selected sections, can put it back together in a VOB file.

SmartRipper also copies the selected tracks. By disabling *Stream Processing*, all tracks are transferred.

> FlasK0.594 has problems when opening such altered VOB files and the resulting IFO files. Thus, it is advised only to copy complete tracks with all chapters and soundtracks, if you want to do further processing with FlasK.

To identify a trailer on a DVD as accurately as possible, you should have an approximate idea of its length, as only that is shown exactly.

In this case, the trailer hides in the second region *vts_04*:

The soundtrack only exists in the English version, as can be seen in the *Stream Processing* tab:

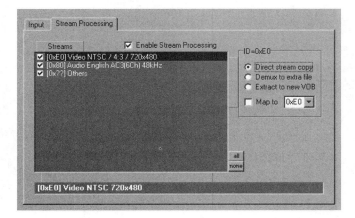

You only have to click on the title in the *Input* tab (as you have already done) and thereby select it.

In the fields below, you can view the exact video stream data:

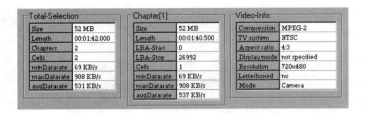

Total-Selection			Chapter[1]			Video-Info	
Size	52 MB		Size	52 MB		Compression	MPEG-2
Length	00:01:42.000		Length	00:01:40.500		TV system	NTSC
Chapters	2		LBA-Start	0		Aspect ratio	4:3
Cells	2		LBA-Stop	26992		Display mode	not specified
minDatarate	69 KB/s		Cells	1		Resolution	720x480
maxDatarate	908 KB/s		minDatarate	69 KB/s		Letterboxed	no
avgDatarate	531 KB/s		maxDatarate	908 KB/s		Mode	Camera
			avgDatarate	537 KB/s			

For example, you can view the *Size* (*52 MB*) and *Length* of the file to be created. Below the first two fields, the minimum, maximum, and average data transfer rates for the video selected are shown.

In the field on the right, the following information is displayed for the MPEG stream: type of compression (*MPEG-2*), the video format (*NTSC*), the aspect ratio of the video image (*4:3*), the resolution (*720x480*) and whether the video image should be *Letterboxed* (*no*).

Before the DVD data can be read, you must decide where the file will be saved. Select the desired directory by clicking on the folder symbol.

The displays next to the selection path always indicate the hard drive resources available:

Once you have selected a title to rip, the *Start* button appears on the left:

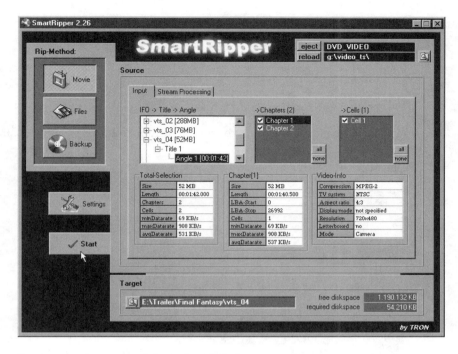

During ripping, a special window informs you of the progress:

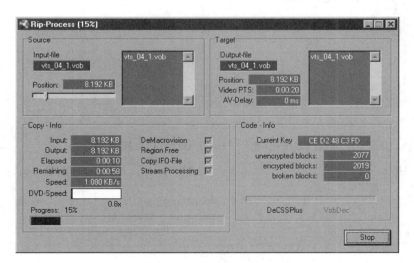

If decryption has not been successful, the following may help:

1 Close SmartRipper.

2 Start your DVD player software: PowerDVD, WinDVD etc.

3 Let the DVD run for a short while.

4 Close the player software, reopen SmartRipper and try ripping again.

After ripping is complete ...

... you will find the desired files on the hard drive:

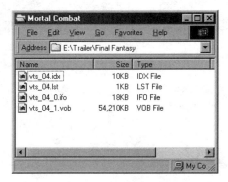

Converting VOB files with FlasK

Up to now, you have only copied the DVD movie files onto your hard drive.

These files with the extension VOB contain both the images and soundtrack of the trailer.

The goal is to convert the trailers into the high-compression format, DivX so that they can then be burned onto CD.

You need a tool to convert these video files from the MPEG-2 format into the format of your choice.

A classic program for this purpose is FlasK, which, like VirtualDub, is small and simple, and available as freeware.

Different versions of FlasK

As any other software, FlasK is also constantly being updated, and there are several versions of the program.

The very popular *FlasKMPEG 0.594* version has been in circulation for some time.

Its successor, *FlasKMPEG 0.6,* is still on the starting blocks. At the time of publishing, there was a preview version available, and we will use it in the following example because the necessary features function perfectly, and we want you to see the new features, particularly those regarding audio.

One (current) significant difference between the two versions is that the FlasK 0.6 shown here will only accept VOB files, whereas FlasK 0.594 can also open IFO files.

The maximum size for a VOB file on a DVD is 1024 MB, thus a movie has to be divided into several VOB files. In plain terms, an IFO file is a list of the VOB files needed to play back a movie.

Thus, FlasK 0.594 can open entire movies and convert sections of them (see the section "DVD sound as a 'radio play' CD" starting on page 173), while you must convert VOB by VOB in version 0.6 and then assemble the individual sections using another program. (In the case of MPEG clips for a (S)VCD, the MPEG tools in TMPEGEnc prove useful with the Merge & Cut function: see page 214.)

Trailers, on the other hand, always fit into a single VOB file and can be processed with version 0.6 and the advantages associated with it.

Processing individual VOB files with FlasK 0.6

After starting the program for the first time, the language has to be selected in *Options*, after which the start screen resembling a media player appears.

The first step in converting a VOB file is to select *File/Open Media*:

The current version of FlasK is not suitable for processing AVIs but can only use MPEG files as original material.

Here, the VOB file of the trailer is selected:

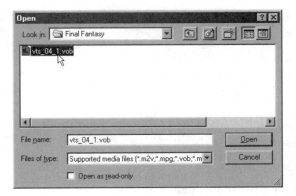

The program analyzes the file to be opened ...,

... and the editing window in which all relevant settings can be made appears:

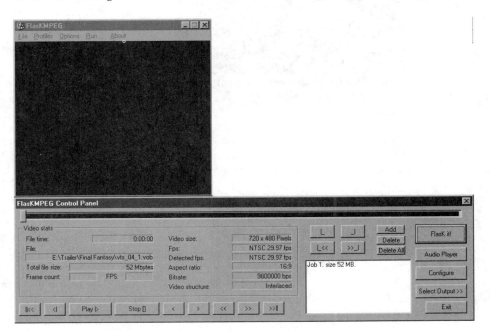

Converting the VOB file proceeds as follows:

Using the controls to view the clip

FlasK has two features for going backward and forward in the clip and for controlling the exact position.

The slider at the top of the window is suitable for rough positioning. For one thing, you can use it to tell whether you have selected the correct clip, or if the clip contains what you were expecting:

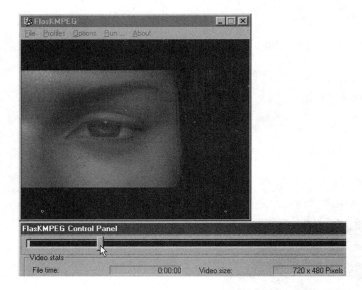

Do not be surprised if this takes a bit of time. As FlasK alone is responsible for displaying the images, many calculations need to be made, which takes time on slower computers and causes delays.

The same applies to the buttons in the lower section of the window:

Even if the *Play* button (third button) usually means the movie is played back in real time, your PC may only do so if it is capable of it.

Otherwise, the movie runs as fast as it can, which for "ancient" 233 MHz processors means that there may be a two-second delay between frames, if the output is reduced to 352 x 288 pixels. An Athlon processor with 500 MHz can already display 5-7 frames per second.

The video file statistics

Between the controls, there is an area where you can view the most important information about the clip, such as the frame size, frame rate or data transfer rate:

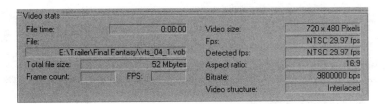

The stack processing option

Even if it's not the case here, it may happen that you don't want to extract the entire movie but rather only your favorite scenes.

FlasK makes it possible to select desired sections of the film and save them in a list as individual *Jobs* so that the program can work on them (perhaps overnight).

This region of the window is needed to determine those sections:

The procedure in brief:

1 Determine where the section begins.

   With the controls already described above (slider and/or command keys), go to the starting point and click on the following button:

2 Determine where the section ends.

Go to the end point in the same way and click to save it.

The section of the movie indicated is shown in the display bar as a black area.

3 Save the job.

Clicking on *Add* saves the new settings as Job 2, and a new, unselected *Job* with its full length (here: 127 MB) appears in the list window:

4 Add another section.

Now you just have to select the new job ...

... and repeat steps 1-3 for it.

Audio settings

If you think that by clicking on *Audio Player*, you can only "listen in on" the video clip, you are wrong.

After clicking on it, a surprisingly large window is launched, containing some options for optimizing the sound for the final product:

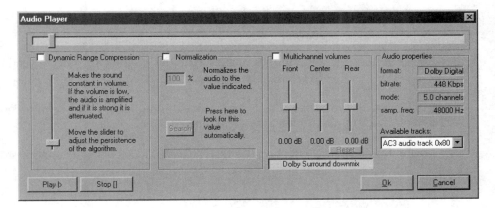

The soundtrack is immediately and automatically played back. You can choose any position with the slider and *Stop* and *Play* the soundtrack.

Information regarding sound and soundtrack selection

On the right, we can select the desired soundtrack with the drop-down menu *Available tracks*:

The data regarding the selected soundtrack is shown in the fields above.

The sound compressor

To make the sound louder, you can use the so-called sound compressor by checking *Dynamic Range Compression*:

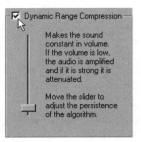

Compressing a soundtrack means that the volume in quieter sections is increased so that the sound seems even.

With the help of the slider, you can determine the level of compression during playback of the soundtrack in real time.

Be cautious, however, because the background distortion also increases and can quickly reach an undesired level.

Normalization of the soundtrack

We recommend normalizing the sound rather than compressing it.

Behind this not very meaningful term hides a volume adjustment by the greatest possible amount, i.e. without over-adjusting it, as this would, without fail, lead to noticeable distortion with digital sound.

You can increase the volume by entering a value in percent, but this is risky business, since in this way, the loudest portions of the movie can quickly exceed the maximally acceptable level of 0 dB.

With *Search*, you can determine a more precise value by automatically searching for the loudest point.

Especially when you want to convert very diverse files – as they are found in a collection of trailers – we recommend that you normalize all clips, as there could be a substantial difference in the sound level between clips.

Mixing channels

Enabling *Multichannel volumes* facilitates increasing or reducing the volume of individual channels, whereby the volume ratio between music and speech may be improved.

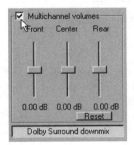

Clicking on *Dolby surround downmix* creates a soundtrack compatible with the Dolby Surround format.

Configuring the output

In creating our target format, an AVI file in DivX video format and MP3 sound, the first step is to use *Configure*:

The relevant dialog field has five tabs in which the necessary settings are adjusted:

The Video tab

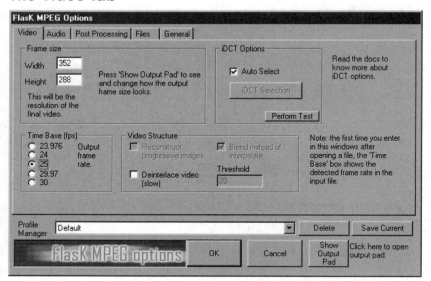

Two entries are important in the *Video* tab.

The clip to be converted into DivX format should be of the highest quality, so the frame size of the original video should be entered into the relevant fields:

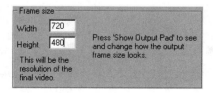

The frame rate, called *Time Base* in this case, should also correspond to the frame rate for playback on a PC.

When producing (Super) video CDs, the video standard (29.97 fps with NTSC or 25 fps with PAL) must be retained.

The Audio tab

Here the soundtrack can be adjusted in two ways:

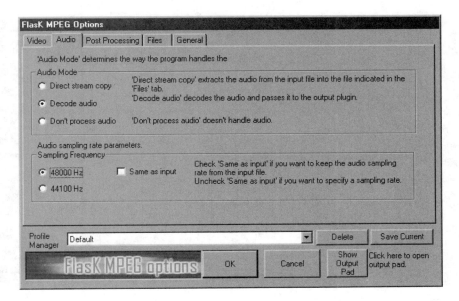

1. If you don't want to combine the soundtrack with the video image, but want to save it as a 1:1 copy in a separate sound file (the path can be set in the *Files* tab), select the option *Direct Stream Copy* in *Audio Mode*. You could then process sound more easily and without loss of quality in other programs.

2. If you want to convert the soundtrack into another format, such as MP3, you must first decode it with FlasK. You absolutely must activate *Decoding Audio*.

Once that has occurred, you can select a *Sampling frequency* between *48000* and *44100 Hz*.

DVD sound naturally has a sampling frequency of 48 KHz, and retaining this value will lead to the least amount of loss.

The Post Processing tab

Normally, the default settings should already be set correctly here:

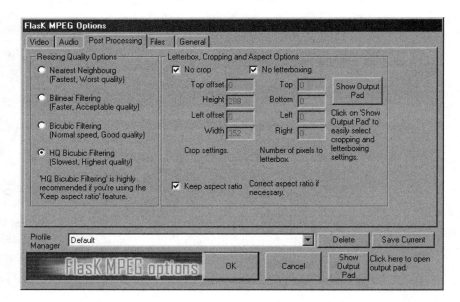

With *Resizing Quality Options*, you can select four different levels of quality. The processing time will naturally depend on the level chosen.

For really good results, select the fourth setting, *HQ Bicubic Filtering*.

As the image is not to be cut or viewed with an artificial border, checkmark the *No crop* and *No letterboxing* options.

The Files tab

Here, you can select where you want the film file to be written to.

The very detailed explanations in this window speak for themselves.

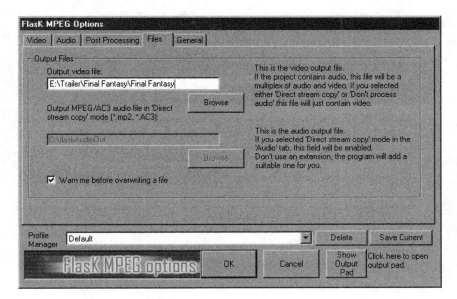

With *Browse*, you can determine the directory and the name of the output file through a file selection box.

If *Direct Stream Copy* was selected in the Audio tab, you can also enter a path for the separate audio file.

The General tab

Leave everything as pre-set:

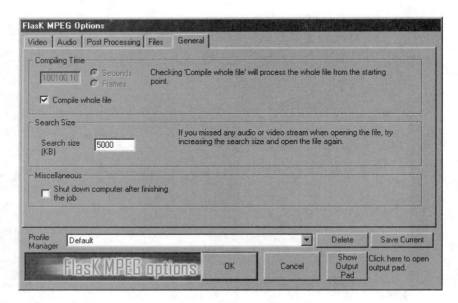

Saving the settings

So that you don't always have to make all the settings again, a way has been found to save them as presets.

Save the current settings with the *Save Current* button located in the lower area of the dialog box regardless of the tab selected.

The entered data is then set as the preset ...

... and can then be activated quickly and conveniently any time:

After all settings have been made and saved, you can leave the configuration dialog box by clicking on *OK*.

The preview screen then becomes considerably larger, as the preset of 352 x 240 pixels in the *Video* tab has been quadrupled to 720 x 480 pixels.

Selecting the codec

Thus far, only the outer elements of the future video have been determined: frame size, frame rate, etc.

The internal values are also of great importance:

The codec used determines the overall file size and picture quality; of course, the aim is always to produce a small clip with brilliant image quality.

A codec is a type of encryption program that will compress the frames. You will find more about codecs and their installation on page 53.

Back in the *Control Panel*, the next step is to select the output format.

To create a video with an eligible codec, you must select *AVI* as the overall format by using *Select Output*:

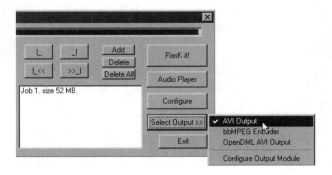

In the same menu, with go to *Configure Output Module* ...

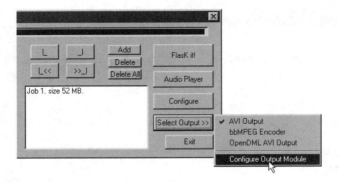

... to launch the dialog box for selecting the codec:

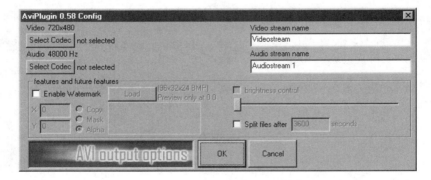

To select the desired video codec click on the higher of the two *Select Codec buttons*:

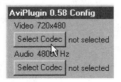

A selection box appears that lists all the codecs installed on your system. The desired format (DivX in this case) is selected:

Most codecs facilitate setting different quality levels. The relevant dialog window opens, if available, by going to *Configure...*:

With the DivX codec, a level-free quality setting is possible. With the slider, you can turn up the data transfer rate to 6000 KB/sec. There is no "correct" data transfer rate, as the result depends on the content of the movie to be converted. The following is generally true: the more motion or frame changes in the movie (e.g. action movies), the higher the data transfer.

For longer movies, we recommend that you convert a small section with a lot of motion using different data transfer rates to find the appropriate setting for the time-consuming conversion of the entire movie. For our example, we have decided on a 4000 KB/sec bit stream, which gives good results:

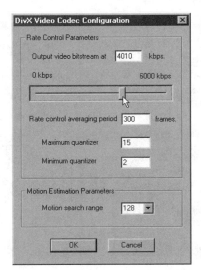

All other values remain unchanged.

After clicking on *OK* twice, we are again in the *AVIPlugin* window, where we click on the lower *Select Codec* button:

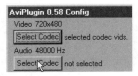

Again a window appears for selecting the audio codec installed on the computer from a list:

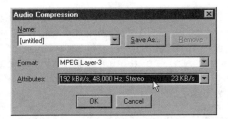

Under *Format*, select the MP3codec. It should compress the sound with a data transfer rate of 192 KB/sec, providing almost loss-free sound. Here, too, we advise testing different data transfer rates to determine how much the file can be compressed.

The occurrence of audible losses depends heavily on the original material. For music to be played back well, you should not reduce the rate below 192 KB/sec. Especially with solo instruments you can hear when compression has been too severe. After clicking on *OK*, you can leave the *AVIPlugin* window so that you can see the Control Panel again:

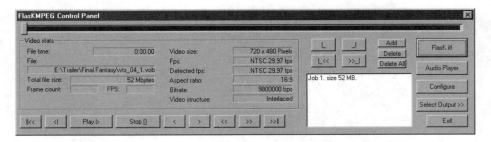

FlasK It!

After all necessary settings have been made, you only need to begin the conversion.

Click on *FlasK it!* ...

... to start the show.

During conversion, the frame currently being processed is shown in a preview window:

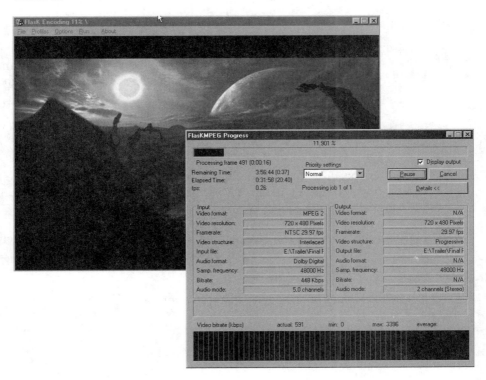

You can disable this display if you would rather do without it:

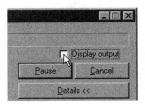

This saves valuable computing time (approximately 15%), which is noticeable right away and can save hours with long movies.

Even if the display option has been disabled, you can still see all the important information:

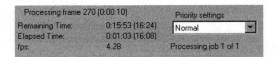

- *Processing frame* indicates the frame currently being converted.

- *Remaining Time* shows an estimation of the remaining time of the process, and even shows (in brackets) what time the process is expected to end.

- *Elapsed Time* is the time elapsed; in brackets, you can see the start time.

- *Fps* shows the processing speed in frames per second – in this case, 4.28, which is a fifth of the normal video speed of 25 fps. – A one hour video with these settings will require more than five hours processing time.

- In the drop-down box *Priority settings*, you can allocate more processor power to FlasK, and give it priority over other system processes. This is virtually unnoticeable, however, so it can be left alone.

With the settings used here, a trailer of 3 1/2 minutes is approximately 128 MB. On the other hand, you do get a video in full resolution approaching a DVD in terms of quality.

16-18 minutes of video in such a resolution can be stored on a CD.

A whole movie on one CD?

The amount of video you can save on a standard CD depend mostly on the two parameters frame size and data transfer rate, which are closely linked:

Regarding quality, the original settings of DVD files of 720 x 480 pixels are naturally the maximum. At the same time, they require a high data transfer rate to be able to save the vast amount of image information. If the data transfer rate is set too low, the artifacts (visible image distortions) are increased so much that the film is difficult to enjoy.

If you halve the values for frame height and width, you get a frame size of 360 x 240 pixels, corresponding to a quarter of the original. This low resolution requires a correspondingly lower data transfer rate.

To get an accurate reply to the question "When does a movie fit onto a CD?", it's worth putting the cart before the horse, by determining the ratio between the space available on a CD – 650 MB – to the number of minutes that can be saved.

A movie 100 minutes in length represents 6.5 MB (equivalent to 1024 x 1024 x 6.5 = 6,815,744 bytes) for one minute of video.

Roughly estimated, a second is 113,000 bytes, which is 904,000 bits, thus around 900 KB.

In other words: a movie 100 minutes in length should only be created with a total data transfer rate (i.e. calculating both frame and sound) of approximately 900 KB to burn it onto a standard blank CD.

To be on the safe side, and not to have to use another CD for just one remaining minute of the video, you should reduce this by at least 10%, thus approximately 800 KB/s.

The frame size therefore determines the size of the area that is required to save the data in question, so that although the previously mentioned 1/4 resolution of 360 x 240 pixels loses some of the quality, this is made up for by making four times the space available to provide detail for the video image, which is particularly good for action scenes.

To spare yourself these calculations, there are several programs available to aid you.

Bit rate calculator

Of the bit rate calculators available, we are using "DVTool" which you can find on the bonus CD or at the following Web address: http://www.musclesoft.de/~combatman/

Using it is easy; you only need to enter ...

1.   the length of the movie to be saved

2.   the audio format

3.   the capacity of the CD-R

     ... and ...

4.   the number of CD-Rs

     ... to obtain the bit rate.

In practice, it looks like this:

DVTool appears like this after starting:

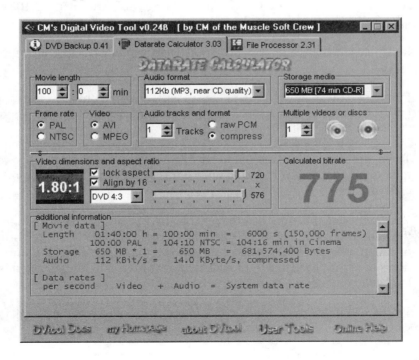

The base values for the above guesstimate were already entered.

1. In *Movie length*, the movie length can be set in exact minutes:

2. The audio format can be selected from the drop-down list *Audio format*. Be aware of the difference between *KB* (Kilobyte) and *Kb* (Kilobit), as 1 byte is made up of 8 bits.

3. In the list you can select from the different CD capacities:

4. The settings for the number of blank CDs to burn is hidden behind a tiny button ...

    One click, and a completely new display will appear:

At the extreme right, you can determine the number of CDs.

On the left, determine the video standard (PAL or NTSC) and video format (AVI for DivX movies, MPEG for (S)VCDs), in the middle, the number of soundtracks (usually: *1*) and whether these should be compressed or not (raw PCM) in the video file.

The end result is a bolded number in the line at the bottom. DVTool determines that an average bit rate of 759KB/s is required to burn a 100 minute movie onto a CD.

DVTool also uses a safety margin for the exactly calculated value.

The settings for the frame size on the left are of no consequence when calculating the bit rate and do not alter the result.

4.2 From DVD to VCD with FlasK

The quality of DivX codec variants is formidable, but playback of the files is (still) restricted to PCs.

If the trailer CD is to play on a standard DVD player, another route must be taken.

FlasK is an excellent tool for burning your DVD movies onto video CDs or even Super video CDs.

You can create "offspring" of your valuable discs in this way that you can let your kids play with.

Additionally, the CDs have fixed standards and can be played back for years to come.

The following steps relate to a movie trailer that was already copied onto a hard drive with a program like SmartRipper, as described on page 128.

Start FlasK, and go to *File/Open* to open the VOB file of the trailer:

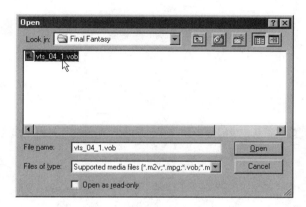

When you open FlasK, you will see the Monitor Window. The Control Panel will also open (you can find a more accurate description on page 142)

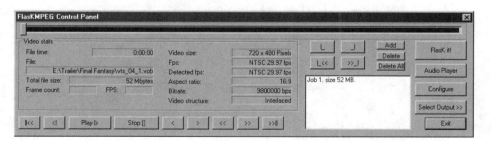

Compared to the very flexible DivX format, there are very specific requirements for frame size and data transfer rates with (S)video CDs (as there are standards to adhere to), to which you should conform.

Audio settings

Behind the *Audio Player* button, there is a useful tool hidden for adjusting the sound to the best level.

You can take on the settings without restrictions, as described in detail on page 142 under *Audio settings*.

Configuring the output

The settings for frame size and sampling rate for the sound are important "frame conditions" for a standard format.

Click on *Configure...*:

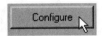

The corresponding window, *FlasK MPEG Options*, makes it easy for the user:

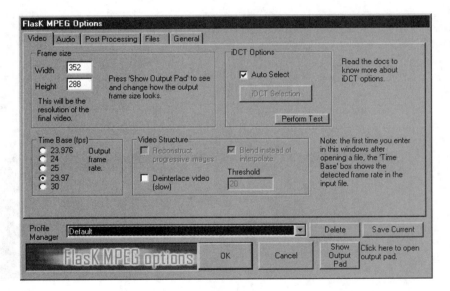

At the bottom of the *Profile Manager*, there is a drop-down menu where you can select the desired profile (in this case, to burn the trailer onto a video CD):

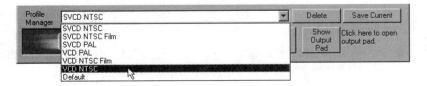

Now you can close the *Options* window by clicking *OK*.

Setting MPEG as the output format

Compared to DivX formats, the video files for producing video CDs cannot be in AVI format but must rather be in MPEG format.

With *Select Output*, the freeware encoder *bbMPEG* included in FlasK can be selected as the output mode:

BbMPEG encoder settings

As opposed to AVI format, the parameters for the bbMPEG encoder are directly set before the conversion.

Click on *FlasK it!* to open the overview window for the MPEG encoder:

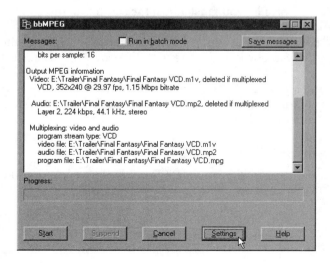

Clicking on *Settings* brings you to the configuration menu:

The General Settings tab

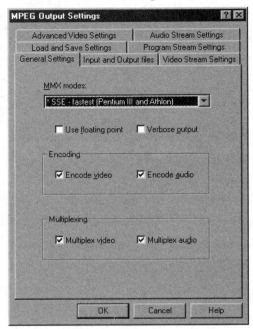

To create a video CD profile, you must adjust the settings in three of the tabs.

In the tab that opened first, *General Settings*, the encoder can be synchronized with the processor, whereby the software usually recognizes the correct CPU.

The *Encoding* and *Multiplexing* boxes should be checked. They ensure that the video and the soundtrack in MPEG format are transferred together, meaning they are interwoven in a stream (multiplexing).

The Video Stream Settings tab

In *Video Stream Settings*, clicking on VideoCD in *Video type* creates a video stream in video CD format:

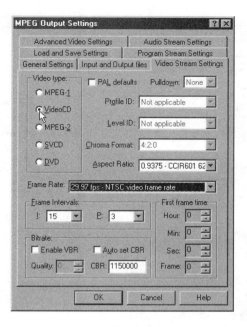

The Input and Output Files tab

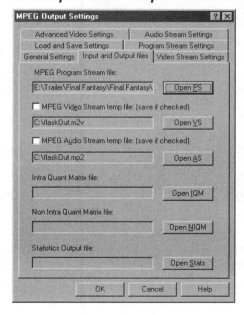

If the bbMPEG encoder is used, it is also responsible for saving the output file.

Under *MPEG Program Stream file*, determine the location and name of the file; everything else can be ignored.

If the temporary MPEG image and MPEG sound files should not be deleted after encoding, so that you can perhaps process them further with other programs, you must check the option and give a file path for the directory of your choice.

The Load and Save Settings tab

The settings you have made can also be saved under an appropriate name by clicking on *Save Settings*:

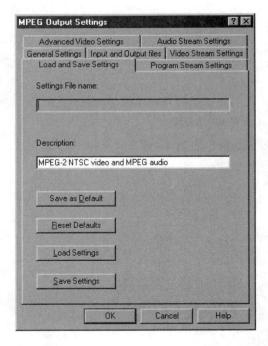

Start the encoding

After the settings have been confirmed with *OK* in *MPEG Output Settings*, you only have to click on *Start* to begin encoding:

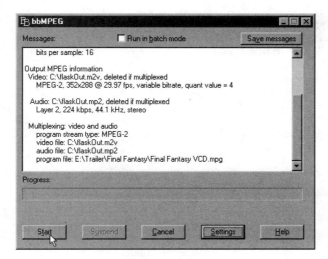

After computing the MPEG files (3 1/2 minutes of material require approximately 15 minutes with an Athlon 500 MHz), bbMPEG does the rest by first encoding the sound ...

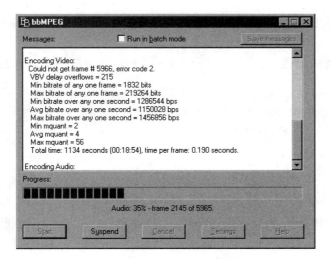

... and then the image and sound stream into a so-called program stream (multiplexing).

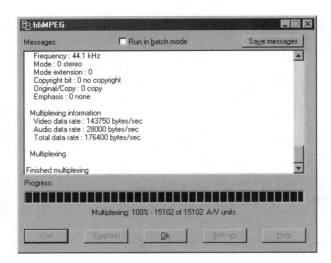

Close the encoder with *OK*.

The MPEG file created (and other files) can be burned as a video CD (see chapter 7).

4.3 Integrating other encoders into FlasK

As we have already seen in previous chapters, to create MPEG files with FlasK, you do not need a codec, but an encoder, i.e. a complete converting program, and one which is supported by FlasK.

This encoder must be a *plug-in*, i.e. not an independent program but a supplementary one.

In this form, it can be incorporated into other programs, such as video editing and animation programs, for processing image files into an MPEG stream.

Other MPEG encoders – different results

Previously, we have used the bbMPEG encoder integrated into FlasK that produces acceptable images.

There are many MPEG encoders available as plug-ins from different manufacturers, and each one creates MPEG files differently, thereby causing the results to vary from encoder to encoder – above all in the computation time.

Here are the most well-known encoders:

- **Panasonic MPEG-1 encoder (Panasonic Digital NetworkServe Inc.)**
  - Is available as a plug-in (for the editing software Premiere), and as an independent program.
  - Creates very good MPEG quality with softer images.
  - Is available as a demo over the internet.
  - Price of full version: approx. US$ 80.
  - At www.networkserve.co.jp/mpeg/index_e.html

- **Ligos MPEG-1/MPEG-2 encoder (Ligos Corporation)**
  - Available as a plug-in (Premiere) and stand-alone version.
  - Very high encoding speed with good image quality.
  - Demo version available on the manufacturer's homepage (can encode up to 60 seconds)
  - Price of full version: approx. US$ 400 (Suite with stand-alone version and plug-in), US$ 180 (plug-in only)
  - At www.ligos.com

- **CinemaCraft MPEG-2 encoder**
  - Available as plug-in and stand-alone program.
  - Available as a demo over the Internet.
  - Price of full version: from US$ 250 to several thousand dollars.
  - At www.cinemacraft.com

Installation in FlasK

We can't really talk about an installation here, since all you have to do is copy the relevant encoder file(s) into the corresponding FlasK directory.

The Panasonic encoder is often used in Adobe Premiere editing software because of its high image quality. For those who perhaps already have the encoder, they should follow the steps below to use the plug-in with FlasK also (other encoders can be integrated into FlasK in the same way.):

1 Find the plug-in in the Premiere directory.

In the Premiere folder, there is a special directory called "Plug-Ins", in which the encoder files were copied on installation.

With Panasonic, the file to find is named *cm-mpeg-pwi2.5e.prm* (Plug-in Version 2.51).

2 Copy the encoder into the FlasK directory.

The found file needs only to be copied into the FlasK directory:

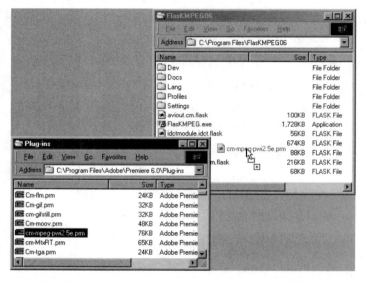

Here the file is moved by holding down Ctrl while moving the file from one window to the next.

3 Renaming the encoder.

So that FlasK can recognize the new plug-in when it's next started, you must give it a comprehensible name.

You can give it any name, as long as the file has the extension ".cm.flask" (e.g. *panasonic.cm.flask*).

4 Controlling in FlasK

If all is well, after a VOB has been loaded in FlasK, you will be able to select the plug-in from the *Control Panel* with *Select Output*:

Settings and features of the Panasonic encoder

The Panasonic plug-in belongs to the most well-known encoders for creating high quality MPEG-1 files for video CDs, which we will address briefly here and concentrate on the most necessary details.

Video CD settings

All parameters for configuring the encoder are located in one window. In FlasK, launch the *Control Panel* by going to *Select Output/Configure Output Module* or by going to *Options/Output format* in the preview screen.

Actually, you only need to select *VideoCD/NTSC* from the *Stream-Format* menu.

For VCDs in the PAL standard, there is the alternative *VideoCD/PAL*, and for personal MPEG-1 creations, *MPEG1*. The latter facilitates using other data transfer rates to create XVCDs (explained on page 189).

For original material with little motion, you can use *Motion Compensation* and the setting *Full Pell* for a sharper image. With motion-packed clips, this may lead to block patterns in the image, so it is advised to proceed with caution regarding this option.

In the *Image Filter* field, you can match the color characteristics of either your *PC* or *TV*. It is advised to create a small test file for both settings and to burn them as VCDs to determine the best option for your DVD player.

Noise Reduction and *Video Filter* can be tested with noisy video clips but should usually be set to *None*.

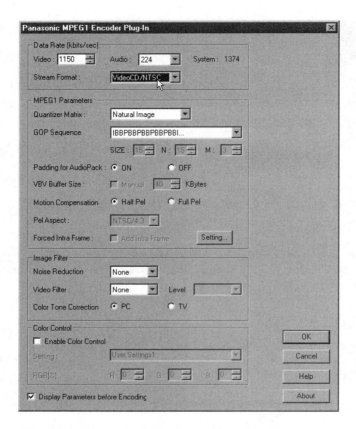

All other settings should be left as they are.

The problem with "packet size" ...

As simple as the configuration of the Panasonic encoder is: the video CD files created with it cannot be used in burning programs like Nero or WinOnCD without further manipulation.

Should you still do this, you may get a different effect during playback on a video CD-compatible DVD player: usually, there is some choppy playback after a little while. Image and sound can also be completely out of sync; in extreme cases, the movie will even stop.

Thus, many annoyed users may have given up after "toasting" a considerable amount of test CDs of different makes.

The fault lies with the encoder, or, more exactly, with the "packet size", an internal value that determines how large the packets created from image and sound files should be.

If the value for the packet size does not correspond to the necessary value of 2324 for video CDs, the aforementioned difficulties may occur.

... and the solution

The packet size problem may sound difficult, but you do not have to denounce the quality of the Panasonic encoder, as this problem can be easily solved.

"Remuxing" is the magic word and is short for "re-multiplexing".

"Multiplexing" is nothing more than interweaving image and sound into one video stream, exactly what the Panasonic encoder did with an incorrect packet size.

Programs like the TMPEGEnc encoder described in the next chapter divide a multiplexed video stream into its original components. i.e. de-multiplexing.

Then, if you carry out multiplexing using the settings for a video CD, you will obtain a standard, consistent video stream.

The necessary steps are described on page 210.

4.4 DVD sound as a "radio play" CD

DVD sound is mostly found in the excellent AC3format (Dolby Digital), but can only be reproduced by suitable DVD players even if you place no value on the picture quality.

If you want to play a piece from your favorite musical not just at home but also on your car CD player, that is also not a problem.

Next, we will place the soundtrack of an entire movie onto a CD and, as movies are usually longer than 74 minutes, we will divide it into suitable sections.

"Flasking" AVI sound

For insertion, we will use the FlasK program, version 0.594 (for differences between this version and version 06, see page 137) and the aforementioned VirtualDub.

First, open the desired movie by going to *File/Open DVD File*:

If in FlasKMPEG 0.6 you could choose VOB files, in version 0.594, the VOB files of a movie are automatically loaded with IFO files. You can only guess which IFO file is the right one, if a copy of the entire DVD is on the hard drive. Otherwise, SmartRipper can be used to find out more exact information about the files (see page 131).

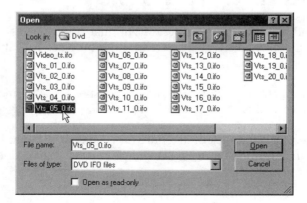

After a lightning fast analysis, the available tracks appear.

We have selected the original version:

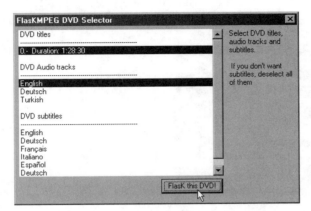

Now you must set the correct format in which the movie has to be converted.

We only want the sound, but FlasK always creates a movie, for which reason you must reduce the image part to a minimum, as it is created only *pro forma* and should not take up a lot of space.

Under *Options/Select Output format*, we will select *AVI Output* as the general format:

Such AVI format is made up of an image and a sound section whose codecs can be freely selected (more about codecs can be found on page 33).

The selection for this combination can be made under *Options/Output format Options*:

First, we select the video compressor with *Select Codec*:

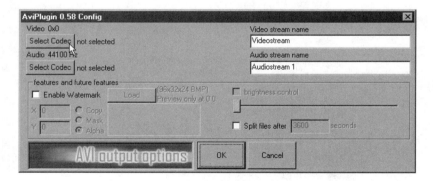

You can reduce the image data to a minimum in two ways.

You can use a codec like DivX and decrease the data transfer rate (quality) to a minimum. The frame size to be used is then of no consequence, as the space required will be determined exclusively by the codec.

We will take the other route and simply set the frame size to the lowest possible value. The codec used then plays a minor role so that even uncompressed full frames can be used:

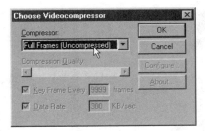

Of more importance is the selection of the audio format:

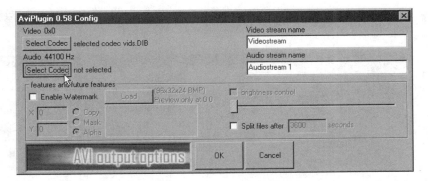

Under *Format*, you absolutely must select *PCM* with *44.100 Hz, 16 Bit Stereo*, so an audio CD can be directly created by any burning program:

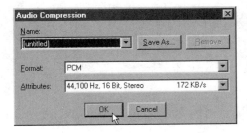

Back in the main window, we now come to the *General Project Options*:

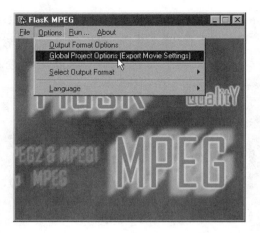

In the first tab, *Video*, the smallest possible frame size of *16x16* pixels is determined:

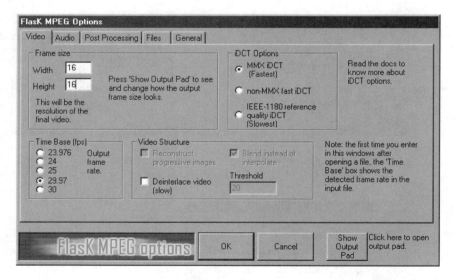

So that the sound is converted in the same format as previously, we need to decode the audio stream, which must be indicated by check marking *Decode Audio* under *Audio Mode*:

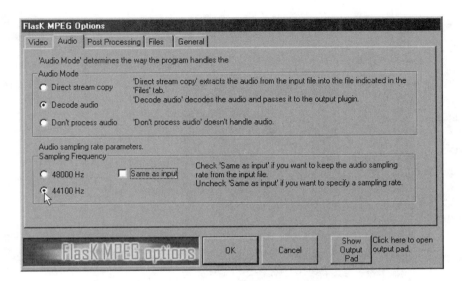

Additionally, you should disable *Same as Input* and set *44.100 Hz* as the *Sampling rate*, otherwise the sound will stream into the future AVI file with the original sampling rate of 48.000 Hz, even though we have selected an audio compression of 44.100 Hz.

Now, only setting the path and name of the AVI clip in the *Files* tab remains:

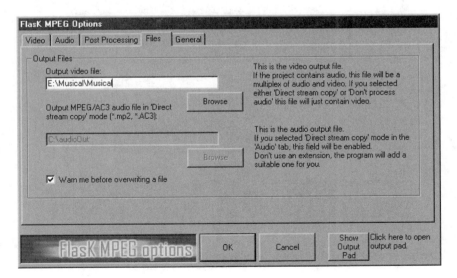

All settings are accepted by clicking on *OK*.

Run.../Start Conversion begins the procedure:

Depending on the computer, converting a movie can take a few hours:

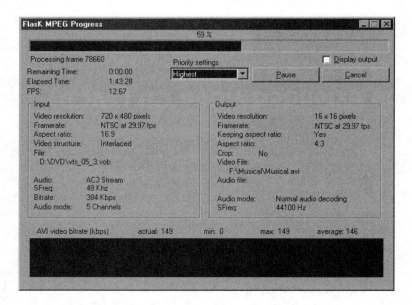

The result is a movie with the smallest image size possible.

FlasK has served its purpose and we will now change to another program that served well in the first section of this book...

VirtualDub: from AVI to WAV

We now have the desired sound in CD format – albeit in an AVI file, together with thousands of tiny video images.

The universal functions of the freeware classic VirtualDub will help our cause further.

Open the converted movie by going to *File/Open video file*:

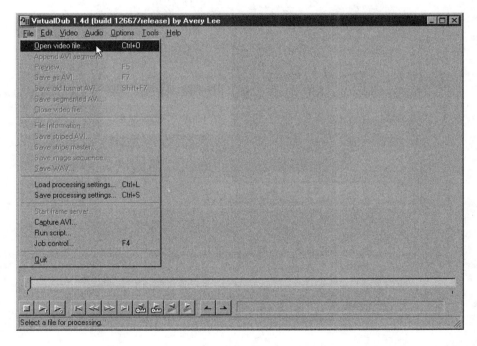

The images from our movie appear inconspicuously in the upper left corner.

With the help of the slider, you can look through the whole movie:

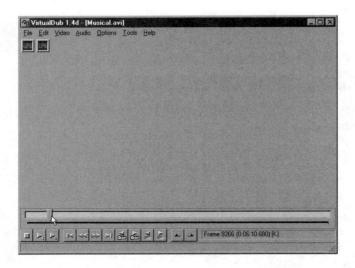

Increasing the volume

Creating AVIs with FlasKMPEG0.594 means that the Dolby Digital stream is re-produced at a lower volume level. FlasK06 offers a normalization option for this (see page 144).

In VirtualDub, you can also increase the volume of the whole clip.

So that any adjustments can be carried out with the sound, the *Full Processing Mode* option in the *Audio* drop-down menu should be selected:

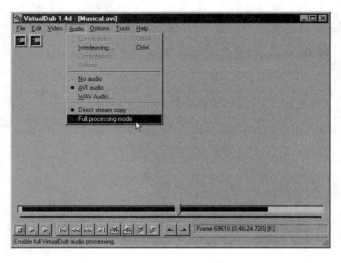

Then the *Volume* option appears:

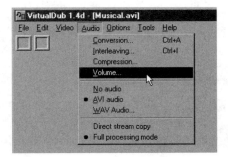

Usually, the volume level can be increased considerably:

Should sound distortion occur during playback, the level can be reduced at any time.

Cutting up clips

It would be easy to save the entire movie as a WAV file, but the output file is almost 90 minutes long and will not fit onto one CD, which only has a maximum capacity of 80 minutes.

The file must therefore be cut up.

This is done by marking a relevant area and then saving it as a separate file.

You can use the slider to control the starting point of the selected area. The buttons at the bottom can be used to determine the exact position:

Aside from the *Stop* and *Play* buttons, the buttons with double-headed arrows are very useful here for step-by-step progression through the images.

These buttons must be used to set the start and end point of the selected area:

It is important to set the playback arrow directly at the selected start or end point in order to find the ideal position by repeated playback and modification. The commands *Move to selection start* and *Move to selection end* can be found with others in the Edit menu.

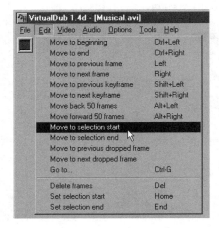

To do a simple "fitting" for burning an audio CD, the end point of the first section must not exceed the maximum size for a CD, i.e. 74 or 80 minutes.

Here, the first section ends after almost 73 minutes and is marked black after the end point is selected.

Now the sound of the movie can be exported into a new file via *File/Save WAV..*:

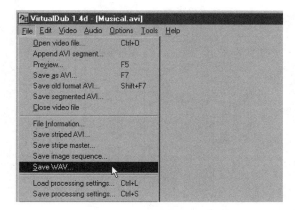

To mark the rest of the movie, simply go to *Edit/Move to selection end* to go to the previous endpoint and make it the start of the second part with *Edit/Set selection start*, the endpoint of which still has to be marked.

This second file also will be output as a new WAV file.

The sound clips can then almost immediately be burned onto an audio CD with a burning program.

5. Converting into a VCD, SVCD or XVCD

Even if it was a little slow to catch on at first, DVD has now become enormously widespread. DVD players can now be bought even at the supermarket and are reasonably priced, thus it is only a matter of time before the VHS cassette will be forced off the market.

Those who think that these players only support pre-recorded DVDs or those created on expensive burners are wrong.

Usually, the technical information supplied with such players includes information on other supported formats, to which hardly any attention is paid, however.

Almost every DVD player can play back video CDs (VCD) – and some even support the Super video CD (SVCD) format.

It all started with far-eastern brands of DVD players with unusual names (e.g. "Yamakawa").

Their particularly low price and ability to play VCDs, SVCDs, and other non-standard formats encouraged computer freaks and movie enthusiasts to try to create their own video CDs and push the technical boundaries.

In the meantime, manufacturers of burning programs have recognized this trend, and thus the VCD and its relatives have experienced a late renaissance, and for good reason:

- Hardware requirements for both creating and playing back CDs are not that high. CD burners are mass produced, just like blank CDs.

- Home video has now become digital thanks to high-quality images from MiniDV: the best output material when saving onto CDs.

- MPEG-1, as used with video CDs, has become standard in the PC domain, and any current Media Player can support it.

The big plus of these often overlooked formats is that they can be created inexpensively with any CD burner and standard blank CDs.

The alternatives presented separately:

5.1 The video CD (VCD)

The video CD is essentially an ancestor of the DVD.

VCDs allow you to store movies of about 70 minutes in length onto a disc the size of a music CD.

This was achieved with the data compression standard presented by the "Moving Picture Experts Group" (MPEG) and termed MPEG-1. Images as well as sound can be compressed to a fraction of their original size with this compression method.

In Asia, the VCD is regarded as important as the VHS cassette is by us and can be found on every street corner. Even current cinema releases appear on video CDs:

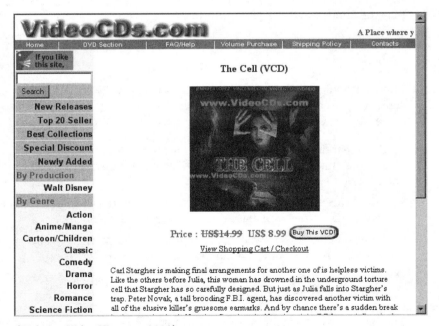

(Website: VideoCDs.com, 2001)

The technical specifications are quite narrowly defined:

- The image resolution is 352 x 240 pixels (NTSC) or 352 x 288 pixels (PAL).

- The data transfer rates are fixed (constant bit rate) and must be 1150 KBit for video stream and 224 KBit for audio stream to support the VCD 2.0 standard.

Uses of video CDs:

A video CD can be created on a blank CD of up to 80 minutes with quality close to that of a VHS cassette.

Video movies can thus be copied from video cassettes onto CDs and played back.

VCDs, rather than video cassettes, provide perfect storage for cartoons. Rewinding and forwarding are unnecessary, and even a child could work the controls.

5.2 The extended video CD (XVCD)

VCDs have very clearly defined specifications. However, some DVD players can also play greatly modified video CDs: the XVCD.

This is not an official format, sanctioned by a consortium, but an independent format that emerged from discussion forums on the Internet, in an attempt to give the extended VCD its own designation.

With this format, the data transfer rate of the MPEG stream does not double but triples, and the frame dimensions can reach up to 480 x 480 pixels.

Consider creating such CDs if your player does not support playback of Super video CDs but you want to have better image quality (naturally, at the cost of running time).

Once more we must say that the only way to find out whether your DVD player supports XVCD playback is through testing them.

Those who would rather not experiment should stick to video CDs or Super video CDs, for they are reliable and will probably still be supported by players in years to come.

5.3 The Super video CD (SVCD)

The Super video CD is an advancement of the video CD.

This new standard was passed by the Chinese national standards committee in collaboration with some electronics companies and should be an effective contrast to DVD.

There are many new features for image improvement:

Instead of MPEG-1, the SVCD uses the "offshoot" format MPEG-2. The concurrent resolution increase to 480 x 576 (PAL) or 480 x 480 pixels (NTSC), demands a higher data transfer rate and results in shorter playing time per disc.

For both the video and audio stream, a variable bit rate (VBR) is possible for SVCD, meaning that the data transfer rate can adjust to the complexity of the video.

Complex image content (action-packed scenes, fast panning) can take up more bits, while images with relatively few changes can be handled more stingily.

Clearly fewer DVD players support this, and those that do hardly mention this fact at all.

Those who want to view short movies as SVCDs should test the different players in the store with a disc burned themselves.

Uses of SVCDs:

SVCD is an ideal medium to save short movies (up to 50 minutes long) on CD in good quality, such as family videos, image sequences, trailers or the best episodes of your favorite TV show.

Here, again, an overview of the specifications for the standardized formats VCD and SVCD:

	VCD	SVCD
Video		
Format	MPEG-1	MPEG-2
Frame rate	25 fps (PAL) 29.97 fps (NTSC)	25 fps (PAL) 29.97 fps (NTSC)
Resolution	352 x 288 (PAL) 352 x 240 (NTSC)	480 x 576 (PAL) 480 x 480 (NTSC)
Bit rate	1.152KBit/s	variable up to 2600KBit/s
Audio		
Format	MPEG-1, Layer II	MPEG-1, Layer II
Bit rate	224KBit/s	32-384KBit/s
Playing time (650MB blank disc)	74 min	30-50min

5.4 MPEG from AVI

Capture programs like VirtualDub or the capture tools supplied with video cards usually facilitate creating AVI files based on the most diverse codecs.

As all types of video CD require MPEG coded video streams, you have to encode the video files, for which you need a suitable MPEG encoder.

There are two kinds of such programs:

Plug-ins can export an entire movie from an existing editing program directly into the desired format.

A stand-alone application opens a movie file, as in VirtualDub, and then encodes it into the MPEG format.

There are some MPEG encoders, but many of them are expensive.

One great exception is the stand-alone encoder *TMPGEnc* from Japan, which is available as freeware and which has more features than most commercial products.

5.5 TMPGEnc – the freeware MPEG encoder

TMPGEnc was originally developed in Japan and could only be used here with an additional program (a so-called patch), which translated all dialog boxes into English.

Its compact size and easy installation facilitated the wide spread of the program. In the meantime it has appeared in a regular English version.

Installing TMPGEnc

TMPGEnc is as system-friendly as VirtualDub, because it doesn't have a setup routine consisting of many files nor does it change any registry entries in Windows. All program files are merely copied into a directory of your choice:

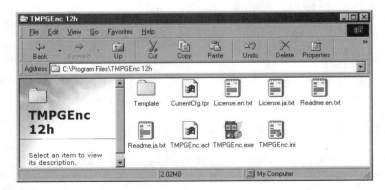

To create a desktop shortcut, simply right-click on the context-sensitive menu to create an icon:

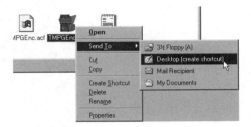

Creating a project in TMPGEnc

Regardless of whether you want to create a VCD, SVCD or XVCD, the basic steps in TMPGEnc are always the same.

The following example deals with converting a short movie file (the sailing movie created in chapter 3 with MovieXone) into the MPEG format for a video CD.

After the program starts, TMPGEnc appears like this:

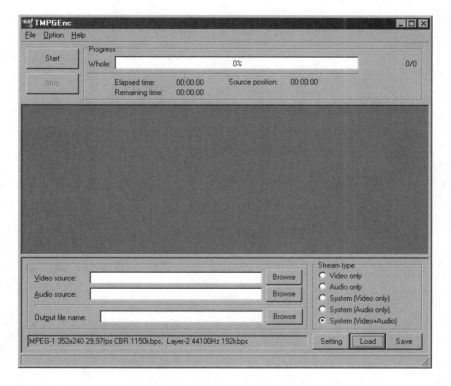

This is how you prepare for the encoding process:

1   In the lower half of the screen, search for the clip from which the MPEG video stream will be created by clicking on *Browse*.

2 Here, we will select the short sailing movie created in MovieXone.

3 In TMPGEnc, the clip appears automatically under both *Video* and *Audio Source*, because the file contains both image and sound data.

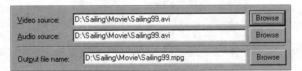

If the encoded movie was created with separate sound and video files, these can also be selected separately under *Video source* and *Audio Source*.

The directory for the MPEG file to be created is automatically determined by TMPGEnc in the *Output file name* field.

With longer projects, it is advised to place the original and target files on separate drives. In this way, the reading and writing heads on the drives don't have to jump back and forth all the time, which shortens the encoding process and keeps the hard drive organized.

4 Now decide whether a VCD or SVCD is to be created and select the required profile. This is no problem, as TMPGEnc is supplied with the most important settings by default.

Click on *Load* to load the desired profile:

If all TMPGEnc files were copied to the same directory, you will get directly into the *Template* folder, where you can find the individual profiles.

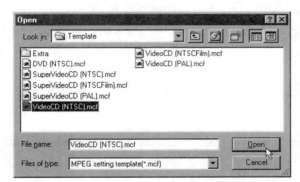

Here a video CD is to be created. Because the TV standard in the US is NTSC, you must select the corresponding NTSC version of the profile.

After the selection, the settings details are displayed in the lower part of TMPGEnc's main window:

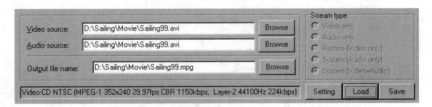

The following can be derived from the display:

1. The data stream created will correspond to the MPEG-1 format.

2. The frame dimensions are 352 x 240 pixels.

3. CBR stands for *Constant Bit Rate* and means that a constant bit rate is used here. Thus, every second of film necessitates the same amount of data, namely 1150 Kbit (the number following CBR).

4. The sound will be compressed with a sampling frequency of 44100 Hz and a data transfer rate of 224KBit per second to MPEG-1, Layer-2. (A layer is a level of compression; here, the second level is used).

Now we can create the MPEG file.

Click on the *Start* button to begin the encoding:

The default settings of TMPGEnc ensure that the encoding process can be followed on a preview screen.

Similarly, in the lower half of the window, the *Elapsed time*, the *Remaining time*, and the current position within the movie clip (*Source position*) are constantly displayed.

After encoding, the MPEG clip can be found in the destination directory and can usually be played back with Windows' Media Player. To create a CD from the movie, you will need a burner that supports this format, e.g. Roxio Easy CD Creator (see Chapter 7).

The quality is quite good and completely adequate for many areas of application.

SVCD instead of VCD

There are essentially two ways of obtaining better image quality:

1. You can experiment with the VCD frame size and data transfer rate to create an **XVCD**.

    Searching for a predefined profile with the *Setting* button will be in vain, as this format is not industry defined and it may well be that your DVD player will play back your XVCD home movies without any problems, while other family members may experience choppy reproduction during playback with their DVD players or may not be able to see an image at all.

2. To avoid running the risk of being eternally dependent on a special device, you should decide upon a standard format, like **SVCD**.

    Such players are few and far between. They are usually low in price and therefore even used as back-up players.

    The SVCD format offers enough options for modification without leaving safe ground. Naturally, there are DVD players that do not support this format, but it is more likely that it will function.

With the *Load* button, you can load a suitable SVCD profile.

Proceed as already outlined for creating a video CD (from page 193).

Creating your own SVCD profile

In many cases, it may be necessary to create your own profile to further increase image quality or eradicate other problems.

Increasing quality by adjusting the data transfer rate

The image quality of a Super VCD can be increased by maximizing the data transfer rate, which may prove beneficial for action-packed scenes.

The predefined profiles in TMPGEnc can only be amended to a certain extent (for example the data transfer rate cannot simply be set as high as you want), thus we have created a new profile for a SVCD with the most suitable variable bit rate for the standard.

All parameters for a new profile are set simultaneously for your own profile creations.

1   With *File/New project* the settings are reset.

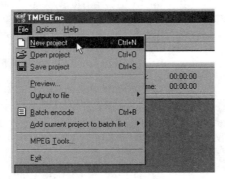

2   Click the *Setting* button to display all parameters and process them.

3   Enter the following values into the corresponding dialog box which is divided into six tabs.

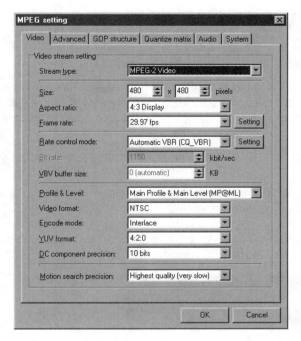

Here are the individual values.

- *Stream type*: the video stream of a Super video CD is based on the MPEG-2 format.

- *Size* standard: the frame size is 480 x 480 pixels.

- *Aspect ratio*: as the output source is TV equipment, the aspect ratio must be 4:3.

- *Frame rate*: set the frame rate to 29.97 frames per second (North American Standard).

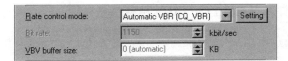

- *VBR* always stands for *Variable Bit rate* and facilitates better use of the data transfer rate by adjusting to the image content. – This setting might be responsible for a choppy reproduction when playing a SVCD, as not all DVD players support VBR.

- *VBV buffer size*: an internal value responsible for buffering the data stream.

- *Rate control mode*: Here the data transfer rate mode responsible for image quality is determined; select *Automatic VBR (CQ_VBR)*.

Click the *Setting* button to determine the lowest and highest data transfer rates to be achieved:

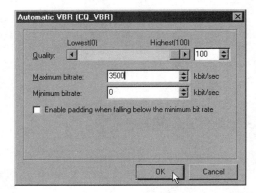

Set the *Quality* to maximum and enter a maximum data transfer rate of 2408 KBit/sec.

The bit rate refers to the sum of image data and sound data stream. The value of 2408 is obtained by taking the official SVCD data transfer rate of 2600 KBit minus the sound bit rate of 192 KBit which is to be set later.

For those who like experimenting, there are no restrictions, and values of over 3000 or even 4000 KBit/sec can be set to test the performance of your DVD player. Such SVCDs no longer conform to the standard.

Let's go back to the actual dialog box:

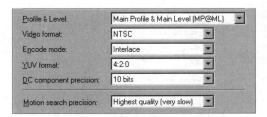

- *Profile & Level*: sets the decoder class and it should always remain at the default setting.

- *Video format*: set the video format to NTSC

- *Encode mode*: if interlace is selected the video images will be created in the interlace format which is typical for TV use (one image consists of two so-called half images which provides a more constant flow motion).

- *YUV format*: this setting affects the data reduction of color components and should always be set to *4:2:0*.

- *DC component precision*: sets the precision during the output process. The highest value is *10 Bit* and provides the best results.

- *Motion search precision*: a principle of the MPEG format is to capture the motion of image components as amendments and save them efficiently. The more precise, the better the image and the longer the calculation will take.

4 The following are settings in the *Advanced* tab:

- *Video source type*: here it is important that you know your video material and whether it was captured in *Interlaced*, or *Non-Interlaced* mode. With TV images or video cards, this is mostly interlaced.

- *Field order*: here the setting to be made depends exclusively on the video material used. With two half-frame video images, the important question is which of the images is to be output first.

- If the incorrect sequence is selected, there may be horizontal flickering movements when playing the SVCD. To resolve this problem, you should select a different entry from the *Field order* pull-down menu.

- *Source aspect ratio*: the aspect ratio of the original material is important i.e. the ratio resulting from dividing the longer frame side by the shortest. If the ratio contains even numbers such as 4:3 in the case of a video with a pixel ratio of 768:576, then the ratio of *4:3* has to be selected (with our NTSC video format).

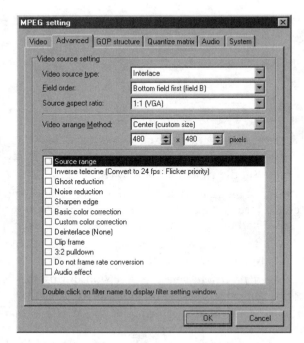

- With 720 x 480 pixels, as it occurs with digital video formats and with all other formats which cannot be divided into ratios containing even numbers, it is suggested to select *1:1 (VGA)*.

- *Video arrange method*: the video obtained can be arranged correctly here.

- It is pretty safe to select *Center (custom size)* and to enter the subsequent frame size (with SVCD 480 x 480 pixels).

5 In the *Advanced* tab: different filters can be configured individually:

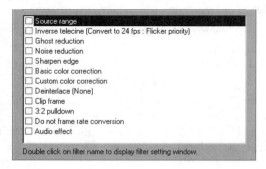

The same procedure applies to almost all of them:

For example, we want to increase the contrast in the movie and eliminate the slight blue cast.

Double-click the filter *Basic color correction* ...

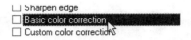

... to open a new dialog box in which you can select any position of the output movie using the slider. Select a favorable movie image to which the filter should be applied:

In the lower section of the dialog box, the parameters *Brightness*, *Contrast*, *Gamma*, *Red* and *Blue* can be defined.

Slightly increasing the contrast and increasing blue and red (the increased red value creates a warmer image) will create an image with strong color, often used in advertising slots.

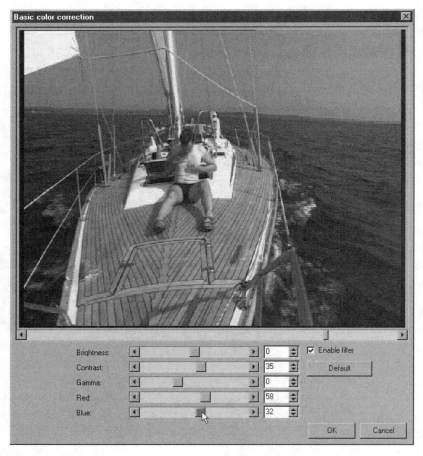

After leaving the dialog box, the filter is automatically activated and is incorporated when creating the MPEG file:

The following is an overview of all filters available:

- **Source Range**

  With this filter a section of the output clip can be selected for encoding so that you do not have to encode the entire clip, which can be very beneficial when testing different settings. Tests with data transfer rates can thus be done on motion-packed scenes.

- **Inverse Telecine**

  Videos in NTSC standard, for instance, always run at 29.97 frames per second, whereas movies in theaters are projected at 24 frames per second. This filter facilitates a frame rate conversion.

- **Ghost Reduction**

  If the same image overlaps itself, a ghost image may appear which this filter can reduce.

- **Noise Reduction**

  Images with strong graininess or high distortion cause difficulties when creating MPEG video; this filter attempts to retain the sharpness of the image as far as possible while smoothing out some flat image components.

  This can provide visible image improvements in case of distorted source material.

- **Sharpen Edge**

  If *Sharpen Edge* is selected, sharpness can be increased without increasing distortion.

- **Basic Color Correction**

  This filter was used in the previous example and affects the image brightness, contrast and color to a certain extent.

- **Custom Color Correction**

  This filter allows you to define contrast ratios or the color of the prospective video to a greater extent than the *Basic Color Correction* filter.

- **Deinterlace**

  Interlaced video clips can be deinterlaced by using this filter.

- **Clip frame**

  First of all, this filter facilitates trimming the image of the output video, sometimes increasing the clipping size. Secondly, the image can also be trimmed maintaining the existing measurements, which facilitates the letterbox effect as it appears in movies played in movie theatres.

- **3:2 pulldown**
  Movies with 24 frames per second can be converted into videos with a frame rate of 30 frames per second.

- **Do not frame rate conversion**
  This filter should be activated to prevent converting the frame rate if the output and prospective formats should be different, which may lead to asynchronous sound.

- **Audio effect**
  Even audio has been given a filter. With Audio effect, the sound can be "equalized", meaning the volume can be increased to the highest level without causing distortion. Also, the sound can be faded in or out at the beginning or end of a movie.

6 Both of the following tabs should only be listed here for the sake of completeness, as they are not normally used.

In the *GOP structure* tab, it is determined how the GOPs, the Group of pictures, should be constructed:

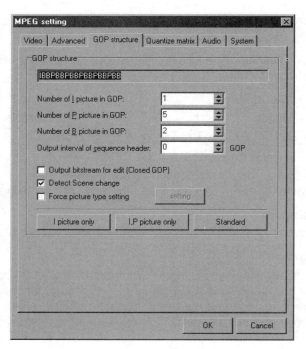

MPEG is a standard that can be very flexible. The principle is based upon the use of so-called delta frames, i.e. not every individual frame is pulled up and compressed, but only changes between frames are saved, saving a lot of space.

At the beginning there is a so-called I frame, which is saved entirely.

Due to this index frame, 17 frames (B and P frames) can be derived if the displayed standard settings are used and only the differences between the images are saved as information. After 18 images, the group of pictures is complete.

Frame number 19 is the index frame for the next GOP.

Because the difference between the last frame and the first frame of a new scene is great, the MPEG standard enables you to terminate the GOP at this point and create a new index frame. This option is enabled by selecting the *Detect scene change* option.

The *Quantize matrix* tab requires great knowledge of MPEG and is best left at the *default* settings:

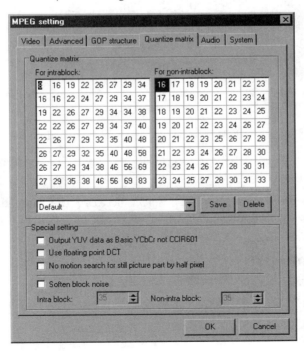

7 The *Audio* tab seems to be more interesting as the settings for the sound of the entire movie are defined there.

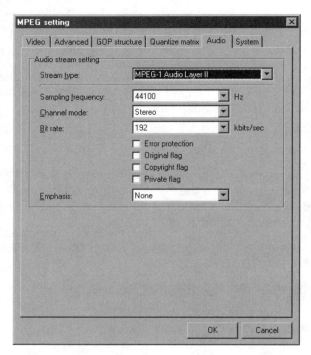

For a standard SVCD, all settings should be made as in the above illustration.

Only the *Bit rate* and *Channel mode* text boxes should be changed:

The data transfer rate for the sound should be between 32 and 384 KB/sec, – a value of 192 KB/sec will generally offer good results.

Under *Channel mode* you can select between the three different stereo channels, each offering a slightly different sound experience:

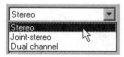

8 Last but not least: the *System* tab:

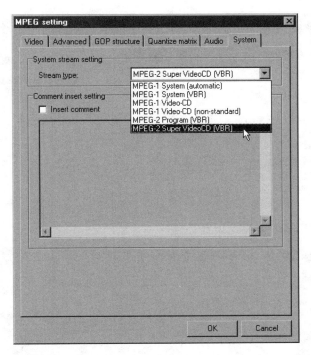

Under *Stream type* we define the type of video stream to be made from video and image components, here: *MPEG 2 Super VideoCD (VBR)*.

Now you can confirm the settings and close the dialog box by clicking on *OK*.

Back in the main window, save the new settings as a new profile by clicking on *Save*. In the future, you will be able to access this profile at the click of a button.

TMPGEnc can help you: remuxing streams with incorrect packet size

We have already described on page 171 how the commercial Panasonic MPEG-1 encoder can be used to create video CD streams.

But the standard clips produced by the Panasonic encoders all have one error: they have an incorrect packet size (see page 172 for an explanation).

The following example shows how TMPGEnc can be very useful in resolving this problem.

Here are the individual steps:

1   Start TMPGEnc and go to *File > MPEG Tools*:

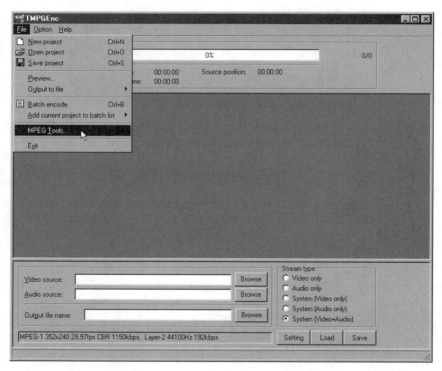

2   In the *MPEG Tools* dialog window, select the *Simple De-multiplex* tab. In the *Input* field use the *Browse* button to search for the MPEG movie created by the Panasonic encoder:

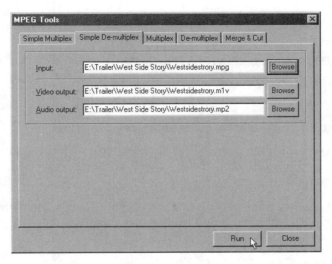

TMPGEnc automatically enters the paths for the *Video* and *Audio output*.

Ensure there is sufficient space on the hard drive. Additional space in the same amount of the source file size is required.

3 Click the *Run* button to start the de-multiplexing. Once the mouse cursor has returned to its normal symbol, the process is complete.

4 Switch to the *Simple Multiplex* tab and select the *MPEG-1 Video-CD* format from the *Type* pull-down menu.

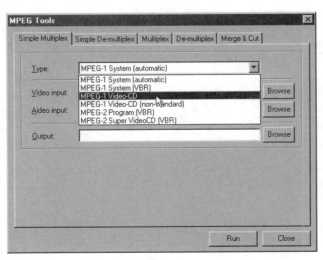

5 In the *Video Input section* use the *Browse* button to select the video-only file which was created by de-multiplexing (extension: *.m1v*).

The corresponding audio file with the extension *mp2* is automatically entered in the *Audio input* field, as well as the prospective target file in the *Output* field.

If you do not want to overwrite the output file, you can simply change the name of it, but you should ensure that there is enough space for another file:

6 Click the *Run* button to start the multiplexing process. Even with large movies this process is finished after a few minutes.

The newly created MPEG file now actually corresponds to the standard of a video CD and will run problem-free on compatible players after it is burned.

6. Compatibility with CD capacity

A standard blank CD has a capacity of 650 or 700 MB. This seems pretty low compared to the capacity of a movie DVD which can be up to 9 GB. Consequently, the maximum playback time of a video CD is 80 minutes whereas a SVCD will reach its limit after approximately 40 minutes.

Files sizes of 1 GB or higher are easily reached if, for instance, a whole movie has been saved on your hard drive using *VirtualDub* and then converted to MPEG-1 format using *TMPGEnc* to create a video CD. The movie has to be split up between two or more CDs and the MPEG file cut accordingly.

6.1 Cutting MPEG files using TMPGEnc

The Freeware encoder TMPGEnc also proves its versatility when post-editing MPEG files.

The Merge & Cut tool offers many options

This inconspicuous tool is actually a small editing program which offers quite a few editing options:

1 Cutting an area

If you are loading only one clip, you can save a cut version by defining a new start and end position. This is ideal if you, for instance, want to get rid of credits or simply want to divide a movie into several sections.

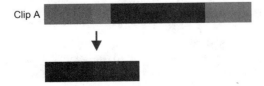

2 **Merging several different movie clip sections to create a new clip**

If you load the same clip several times, a new movie can be created from different sections. This is a good way to remove advertisements.

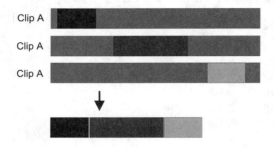

3 **Merging individual clips**

A new movie clip can either be made from a number of small clips or, if desired, only from small sections of individual clips.

A large movie clip is cut

Large movie clips in MPEG-1 format as well as in MPEG-2 format used for SVCDs can be easily cut with the *Merge & Cut* tool. The resulting smaller movie clips will then conveniently fit on to two or more CDs.

The term "cut" is actually not accurate as, in reality, two entirely new clips are produced. Consequently, there always has to be adequate space on the hard drive of your computer.

The movie used in this example was created as a VCD movie and has a length of 1 hour 31 mins and 35 secs; therefore, two blank CDs are necessary to save it completely.

Start TMPGEnc and from the *File* menu select the command *MPEG Tools...*

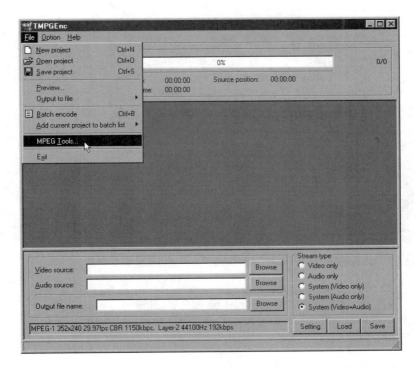

Select the *Merge & Cut* tab from the MPEG Tools dialog box:

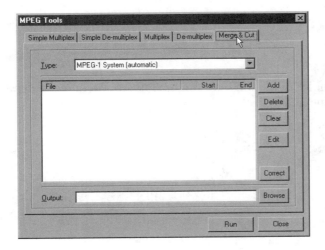

Select the format of the clip from the *Type* pull-down menu – i.e. *MPEG-1 Video-CD*:

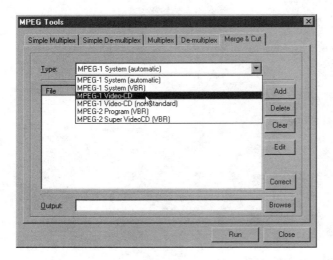

This information is necessary to create clips which will conform to the format. Especially MPEG movies can not be easily cut at any position, as they consist of entire index frames as well as B and P frames, which are derivatives of previous index frames (see also page 207).

Click *Add* to open the MPEG movie to be cut.

Select the movie from the file selection box; the movie title and its file location will appear in the MPEG Tools dialog box:

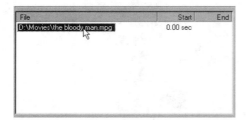

Double-click this entry to open the *Edit merge item* window in which you can edit the clip.

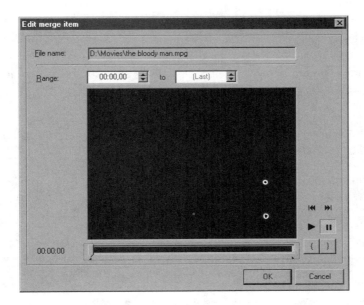

Set a new start and end position for the clip.

The clip is cut as follows: First select the section which will be saved on the first CD. The start of the movie remains the same; only the end of the new movie file has to be set.

Use the slider and the buttons to the right of it to navigate through the movie.

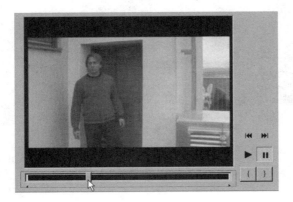

Above the Play and Pause buttons, you will find two buttons with which you can go back or forward frame by frame in the clip:

If you want to obtain two CDs of about the same size, set the end position of the first part of the movie in the middle of the complete movie.

Should the first CD be filled to its full capacity (for instance if you want to add data to the second CD), the end position should be set after 74 or 80 minutes (depending on the size of the blank CD).

For this example, the movie was cut in half. By looking at the movie frame by frame, the exact last frame of the last scene can be found in the editor; however, a precise cut is generally not seen in the final movie clip due to the restrictions of the MPEG format.

Click the *end position selection* button (bracket symbol) at the lower right to save the position. The selected area appears black in the slider panel.

You can close the window by clicking on *OK*. In the clip list, the new end of the clip is displayed as a numerical value (in seconds):

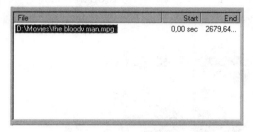

In the *Output* text box at the bottom, assign a name to the first new section of the movie and use the *Browse* button to define the corresponding directory ...

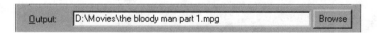

... then click *Run* to begin the copying process.

TMPGEnc keeps you posted of the current status of the copy process:

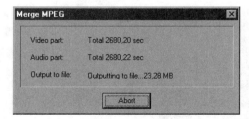

After the new file has been created, you will find yourself back in the previous dialog box.

Double-click the same clip to open it again and to create the second and final section of the clip.

The values set before are still available and very useful for setting a new start position.

Set the slider to the position of the previous End position.

It is very useful if you click on the Mark-In button (open bracket) in addition to the frame-by-frame button to display the exact numeric position in the left *Range* box:

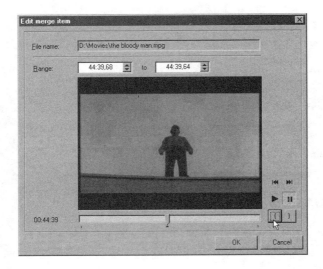

Determining the end position is, on the other hand, carried out very quickly: simply move the slider all the way to the right and click the *End position* button.

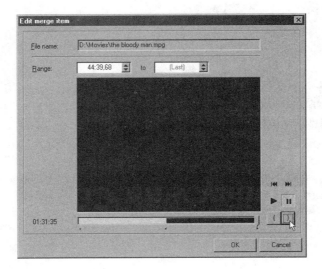

In the second *Range* box, the term *Last* should appear, which ensures you that the clip has been selected up to the last frame.

The second half of the movie has now been defined and only needs to be saved in a file with an appropriate name:

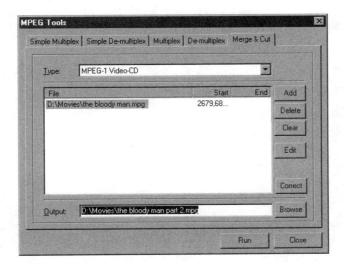

After both sections have been created successfully, the original file can be deleted.

It is also possible to make one movie clip from many small ones

This tool is not only used to cut movie clips.

It can also be used to merge different small movies (or movie sections) to one big MPEG file, provided that they are all the same type of movie files.

In this case, click the *Add* button to add further clips.

7. Burning onto CDs

The results of all your efforts should not remain forever on your computer's hard drive and should therefore be finally saved on conventional CDs.

At the moment, there are two basic methods for saving film files to CD and playing them back:

1. Clips in such formats as DivX can be saved in a standard CD format and can be played back directly on the computer using programs such as Microsoft's Media Player.

2. The format of the video CD comes into question if you wish to make your videos independent from the computer and use a standard DVD player for playback, which requires that the capacity be limited to 80 minutes per disc. To do so, the film files should have been created using a standard conforming MPEG-1 format (see Chapter 6).

The CDs in the first category can be created using any standard burning program which can produce a normal data CD.

With the second alternative, it is a bit different.

Until recently, burning video CDs was an exotic feature that was only offered by some very expensive authoring programs, such as "Videopack".

Using software taken from Adaptec's "CD Creator", Roxio has developed a product for the consumer market which makes creating CD projects easier through a series of Wizards. Thus, it is possible to create simple menus for video CDs without needing a vast knowledge of programming.

> Using menu-controlled (S)VCDs together when playing back in stand-alone players is not without its problems. Not every VCD-compatible DVD player can handle these CD-i features (CD interactive) that were developed years ago. The display may remain black, or the menu might show, but the movie cannot be played back. If your player refuses to play back, you only have one option (other than buying a new player): to forego using such selection menus.
>
> Those who do not yet own a DVD player but place value on the compatibility of VCDs, should do a "practice test" in the store with a self-burned disc.

7.1 Roxio CD Creator 5 Platinum

The goal of the following project is to create a VCD that contains three different short films. After inserting it into a DVD player, a menu screen should appear. Pressing *1*, *2*, or *3* on the remote control will start each of the corresponding films.

Which data is necessary?

Before starting the program, the following "ingredients" should be available:

1. The actual film files

    They should have been encoded into video CD-capable MPEG-1 format.

2. The start sequence (optional)

    This deals with a film that starts directly after the playback of the video CD has started. This is so the actual menu does not just "jump" onto the display, but instead there is a transition from a black display to the menu (effectively a type of intro).

3. The selection menu (optional)

    It must likewise be available as an MPEG film; in the simplest case it is a still picture that was exported from a video editing program. The menu displays the films for the user to select using the corresponding title number on the remote control of the DVD player.

Starting with the Wizard

If the program was installed, it can be started by using the shortcut on the desktop, or by going to the so-called *Project Selector* (right-click on the desktop icon):

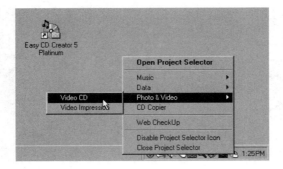

Those who prefer something more visually engaging can choose the first way and select the appropriate project, in our case *video CD*.

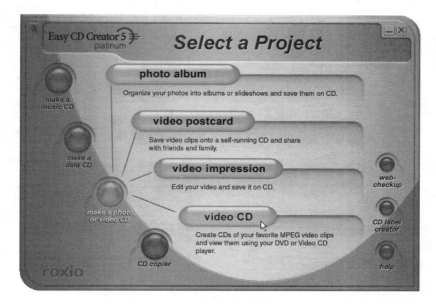

Regardless of what decision you make, the CD Creator Wizard will load in order to make your life easier.

Unlike with most Wizards, the user will be guided through each of the steps involved in creating a CD in a clear and understandable way. Each newly created project can still be subsequently altered.

The very first thing you must do is to decide on the type of CD.

We do not just simply want to stick films one after the other, but rather take the elevated way by using a selection menu. Therefore, we choose the *One Level Menu Structure*:

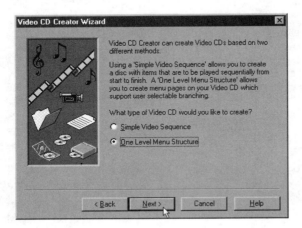

Selecting the film files

The next dialog box allows you to define the film files.

1 You must have at least one film, which requires clicking the *Add...* button at least once:

2 Select the desired MPEG file through the file selection dialog box. The playback sequence for later on is at this time irrelevant.

3 A window for the selected film opens, in which the properties for that clip can be controlled.

The *General* tab provides information regarding the existence of sound and picture. The scrollbar underneath the picture window can be used to move throughout the film to check its contents.

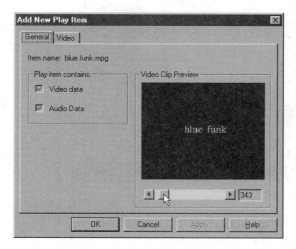

In addition to the file path, the basic film parameters such as format, picture size and length are shown In the *Video* tab.

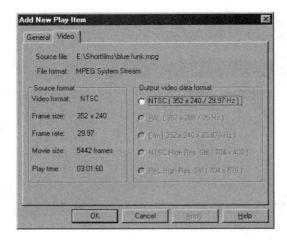

Go through steps 1 to 3 for each additional film to be added.

Once all the clips have been specified, proceed by clicking on *Next*:

Defining the start sequence

Now the start sequence and the menu page have to be determined.

The start sequence in our example is a short film that introduces the menu items bit by bit until the actual menu is created.

We will define it as follows:

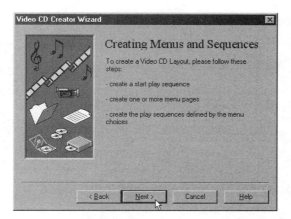

1 All the play items loaded up to this point are shown in the left window. The film to be used for the start sequence is not yet shown and can be added using the *Add...* button.

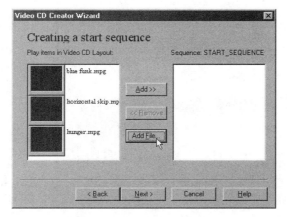

2 The relevant clip gets added through a file selection dialog box.

3 As before, the details about the clip can be seen using the *General* and *Video* tabs.

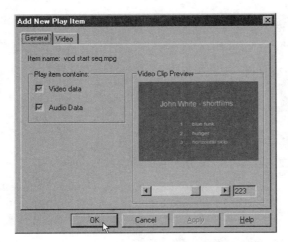

The selected film will then appear in the right window as the start sequence.

If you wish, more clips can be added by repeating steps 1-3 for each clip.

This section is completed by clicking on *Next*.

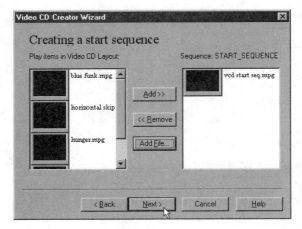

Defining the menu page

Although it is called a menu page, it is an actual film, just like the play items and the start sequence. With a bit of skill and the correct software, you can create an animated menu, and export and encode it into the necessary VCD format with TMPGEnc.

The menu clip's sound track can be used as background music. Since the menu picture is handled in the same way as a normal film clip, it can naturally contain sound which can be played at the same time in the background. Therefore, it is worth considering using a menu clip several minutes long so that the music does not repeat itself too soon.

Those types of clips naturally use as much space as the actual films.

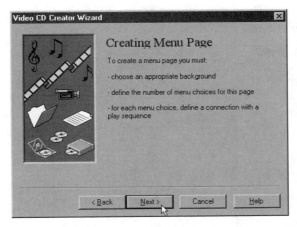

1 The following selection field allows you to go back to the clips previously loaded as well as add new material with *Add from file...*

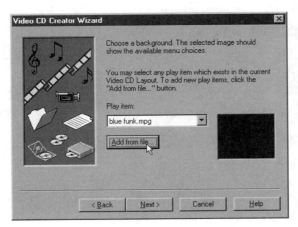

2 In our example, the *vcd menu.mpg* clip contains the selection menu.

3 Naturally, you can also have a quick look at the clip at this point, just to ensure you have chosen the correct one.

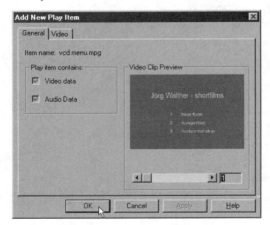

The name of the menu clip appears in the *Play item* field.

After clicking on *Next*, you must decide how many selections will be possible in the menu.

The menu picture you have defined should display the possible selections – in our example, three short films will be available, and therefore the number should be set to *3* in the *Number of menu choices* field.

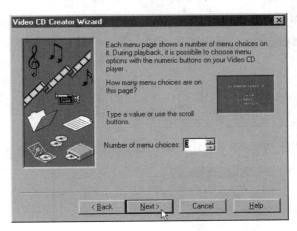

Which number plays which film?

Up to this point, the play items have been imported, but their position in the resulting video CD has yet to be determined.

Therefore, we must now define in the following which number key on the remote refers to which film.

Since we specified three possible selection choices in the previous step, the dialog field in the next window requires us to define the hotkeys (1 through 3) for the play sequences.

1 The first step enables you to give an individual description to each of the play sequences for a better overview. Select the relevant sequence and click on *Edit*.

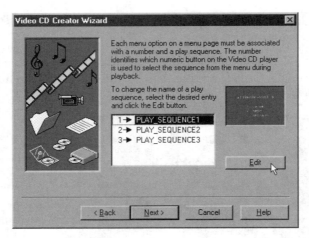

2 As a rule, it is recommended to use the name of the film.

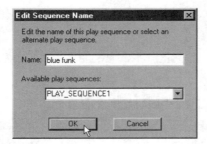

3 After the entry has been made, the changed entry appears in the dialog field.

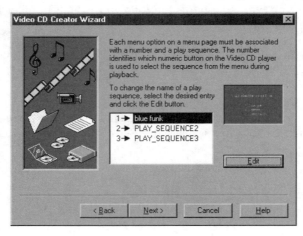

4 Once all the menu items have been named, this section can be ended by clicking on *Next*.

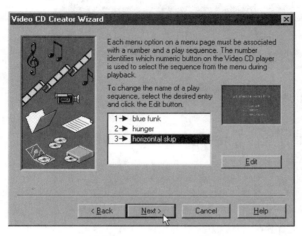

5 If additional menu pages need to be added (for example, to display a selection of three additional films on another page), they can be added in the next window by clicking on *Add Page*.

Adding further menus to our example is not necessary. Therefore, we can proceed by clicking on *Next*.

6 For the first play sequence (the sequence that is played back by pressing *1*), the relevant film can be selected from the list on the left and assigned by clicking on the *Add* button.

It is also possible at this point to include several films for each sequence.

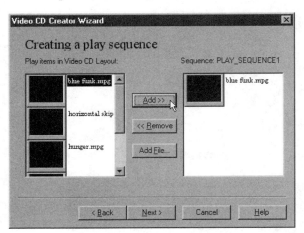

7 Once the sequence has been defined (in this case, only one film), clicking on *Next* will enable you to define the next play sequence.

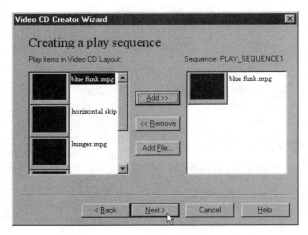

8 Now for the allocation of the next play sequence: The actual order in which the films are to be played will be realized at this point (Pressing on 2 on the remote control should play back the film *Death from Starvation*).

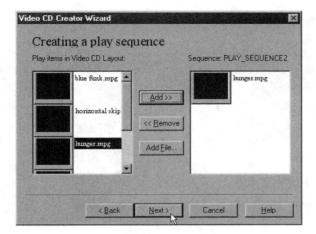

Dress rehearsal

Once all the play sequences have been determined, the work can be viewed with the internal player.

Clicking on *Playback* will start a type of video CD simulation.

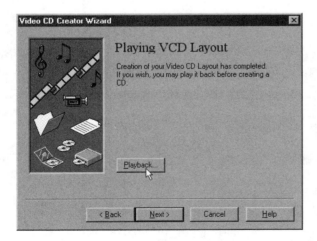

Playback of each of the individual films one after the other is not particularly smooth, but this test is very useful if we are trying to check the menu structure without immediately burning a test CD.

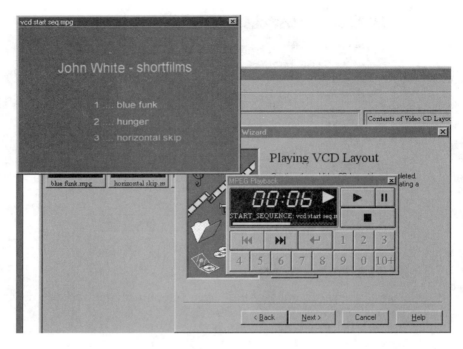

If the virtual CD has passed the test, the last step involved is to select *Create the CD now* and click on *Finish*.

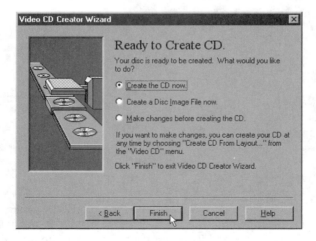

The necessary files will be assembled immediately, and the burner will kick into action.

Index

Index

Index